DATE DUE

JUL 09 1986 +2019	
JAN 2 2 1987	
MAR 8 1987	
APR 9 1987	
SEP 3 - 1987	
OCT . 1 1987	
NOV 2 6 1987	
MAR 7 1988	
NOV 2 4 1988	
MAR - 5 1993	
AUG 0 3 1993	
AUG 2 6 1994	
13T 9 X/ov '94	
FEB. - 2 1996	

HOME BREWED BEERS AND STOUTS

by
C. J. J. BERRY

*Editor, "The Amateur Winemaker and Home Brewer"
and "The Homebrew Supplier"*

*HOW TO BREW SUPERB ALES, BEERS,
LAGERS AND STOUTS FROM KITS, MALT,
MALT EXTRACT AND DRIED MALT EXTRACT*

First Edition 1963
Second Edition 1966
Third Edition 1970
Fourth Edition 1970
Fifth Edition 1981
2nd Impression 1982
3nd Impression 1982
4th Impression 1982
5th Impression 1983
6th Impression 1983
7th Impression 1984

ISBN 0 900841 58 3

Published by:
"The Amateur Winemaker Publications Ltd.,
South Street, Andover, Hants.
SP10 2BU

Printed in Great Britain by:
STANDARD PRESS (Andover) Ltd.
South Street, Andover, Hants.

Cover photograph by Chris Clarke

Design: Cassedy Russell Design Consultants Limited

Photographs: Derek Smith

CONTENTS

"The process of brewing ought to form a part of the domestic economy of every family . . . the greater part of the population of this great and free country are doomed to destroy their health by the consumption of the intoxicating stupefactive compositions of the porter quacks and beer doctors, which are daily passing into their stomachs in the form of pothouse slops or wash, under misnomers of porter, ale, intermediate beer or that nondescript and indefinable compound, London small or table beer."

—William Cobbett.

About this Book

ONE in every 48 pints of beer drunk in this country is brewed at home, according to a recent survey by the Economist Intelligence Unit, and home brewing is now very much an accepted part of the social scene. Kits for brewing excellent bitters, pale ales, stouts and lagers are readily available from specialist shops and from chain stores and people in their thousands, perhaps spurred into the hobby initially by the ever-increasing cost of pub beers, have found that they can indeed with the greatest of ease brew at home really satisfying beers for as little as 7p a pint. Why not join them?

Modern home brewing really "took off" in the 1960's.

In his Budget on April 3rd, 1963, Mr. Reginald Maudling, then Chancellor of the Exchequer, abolished Excise restrictions upon brewing beer at home; no longer was it necessary to have a private brewer's licence or to pay duty upon the beer produced. You are free to brew as much beer as you like, and the only **legal** stipulation that must be observed is that not a drop of it must be sold. At one stroke of the pen Mr. Maudling very sensibly thus gave home brewers the same freedom in the practice of their craft as had always been enjoyed by home winemakers.

There was an upsurge in interest in home brewing and eventually beer kits started appearing on the shop shelves to meet the demand.

But there is much more to the hobby than just making up a kit; home brewers need to know the theory behind the techniques they use, and how to devise their own formulations for any type of beer.

This book, first published that same year, was the very first to cover in detail the home brewing of beers and stouts, and has become accepted as the ideal introduction to the subject. It has been welcomed by the thousands who wanted to brew their own wholesome beer but were at a loss as to how to set about it, and well over half a million copies of the earlier editions have been sold.

"Home Brewed Beers and Stouts" has been continually brought up to date, of course, and this completely revised and improved edition appears in a more modern and attractive format, and gives you not only the background and theory of brewing but instructions and recipes for ales, beers, lagers and stouts of all types, from the lightest lager to the blackest stout, for beers from kits or malt extract, and for "true beers" from barley malt, made by the mashing process. Diabetic beers and "mock" beers are also covered.

Great advances have been made in equipment for producing "Keg" beers as well as bottled, and these are explained in useful detail.

Beer, our national drink, is not only thirst-quenching and enjoyable; it is also nourishing. It is a fact that a pint of strong beer has the same food value as a pint of milk (about 400 calories). Beer is rich in several B complex vitamins and home-brewed beer, especially, is a healthy, unadulterated drink. One often hears the comment that "There's nothing like bread and cheese and a glass of beer," and, strangely enough, it could well be claimed that chemically and nutritionally this is indeed the perfect meal.

Do not be misled by anyone "in the trade" who has a vested interest in commercial beer sales, or by anyone else who tells you that it is not possible to brew an excellent beer using the simplest apparatus, or that home brew is of inferior quality. It is perfectly possible to brew a beer every bit as high in quality as that which can be obtained in your "local", and the more you study the subject the more you will realise why: you are using exactly the same ingredients as the commercial brewer, and similar methods, albeit on a smaller scale; and there is no reason at all why you should NOT succeed, and succeed dramatically. After all, at one time every public house and inn—and many a home—brewed its own beer, and commercial brewing on a massive,

6

"amalgamated" scale is but the product of modern times. There is today a strong trend towards the old system of small breweries and home brewing.

There is great satisfaction in being able to offer a friend a tankard of your own good ale. The economy of home brewing is dramatic, too; its basic cost can be as little as 6 or 7p a pint!

Home brewing is a fascinating and rewarding pastime, undertaken intelligently, and this is the book to set you on the right track. Good brewing!

CHAPTER 2

Brewing Vocabulary

ACETIC ACID:

The acid formed when beer is left exposed to the air and turns vinegary.

ACROSPIRE:

Shoot which grows from grain of barley during malting.

ADJUNCTS:

Grains such as maize, rice or wheat used to supplement the malt.

ALE:

Formerly, unhopped beer.

ATTENUATION:

The drop in a wort's specific gravity as sugar is used up during fermentation.

BARLEY:

Grain most commonly used for brewing.

BARLEY WINE:

A very strong beer. See page 26

BARM:

Mixture of wort and yeast.

BARREL:

In the trade, a cask holding 36 gallons. The home brewers plastic barrel holds 5 or 6.

BEER:

Hopped ale.

BEST BITTER:

A high-quality pale ale. See page 25

BOTTOMS:

Deposits of yeasts and solids formed during fermentation.

BREWERS' GRAINS:

The insoluble residue of malt left in mash tun after the wort has been run off.

BREWBIN:
A six-gallon plastic bin in which the wort is fermented.

BREWERS' YEAST:
A top-fermenting strain of *Saccharomyces cerevisiae*. This yeast ferments on the surface of the wort, forming floating islands of yeast, which subsequently sink. Lager yeast (*S. Carlsbergensis*) is bottom fermenting.

BROWN ALE:
A medium-strength, darker beer. See page 26

BURNT SUGAR:
Old name for caramel colouring: prepared from glucose.

BURTON WATER:
A description applied to water of similar hardness to that found at Burton-on-Trent, important in the brewing of pale ales.

BUSH:
Ancient sign for an inn (hence: "Good wine needs no bush.") Probably of Roman origin; a "bush" of ivy and vine leaves was the symbol of the wine-god, Bacchus.

CALCIUM SULPHATE:
One of the chemicals which gives water a permanent hardness. Popularly called gypsum or Plaster of Paris.

CARBON DIOXIDE:
Gas given off during fermentation which gives the "head" on beer, and the sparkle.

CARAMEL:
See **BURNT SUGAR.**

CASKS:
Butt, 108 gallons; Puncheon, 72 gallons; Hogshead, 54 gallons; Barrel, 36 gallons; Kilderkin, 18 gallons; Firkin, 9 gallons; Pin, $4\frac{1}{4}$ gallons.

CONDITION:
The "life" a beer has owing to the carbon dioxide in it.

CUTTING:
Stopping fermentation by adding finings.

CYTASE:
Enzyme in barley grain which dissolves the cellulose protecting the granule and allows fermentation to proceed.

DEXTRINS:
Substances in wort released during mashing.

DIASTASE:

Enzyme in barley which converts starch to fermentable sugar.

DRAUGHT:

Beer served from the barrel.

DRY HOPPING:

Adding a few hops at the end of the boil to restore lost aroma.

ENZYMES:

Catalysts in the barley grain which affect malting during the mashing process.

See **CYTASE, DIASTASE, INVERTASE, MALTASE,** and **ZYMASE.**

EX-WINE FIVE (or polypin):

A five-gallon plastic container previously used commercially for draught wines etc. Excellent for fermenting or resting beer, using a fermentation lock, but not for storage of a primed beer.

FERMENTATION:

Yeast working upon a sugar solution (the wort) to produce alcohol and carbon dioxide.

FERMENTATION LOCK:

A little gadget to protect the brew from bacterial contamination.

FININGS:

Used for removing suspended solids from cloudy beer: usually gelatine, isinglass or Irish Moss.

FLAKES:

Maize, rice or barley can be used as an adjunct to malt during mashing; it has already been "pre-cooked".

FOBBING:

Overlively beer foaming up out of the bottle. Usually the beer has been kept in too warm a place or has been overprimed, or the bottle has been overfilled.

GALLON:

8 pints, 160 liq. oz., or $277\frac{1}{4}$ cu. inches (American gallon, 128 oz.).
1 Imperial or English Gallon = 1.2 U.S. gallon.
Equivalents:

English	1	2	3	4	5 gallons
American	$1\frac{1}{4}$	$2\frac{1}{2}$	$3\frac{1}{2}$	$4\frac{3}{4}$	6 gallons

GILL:

Usually $\frac{1}{4}$ pint, but in some areas $\frac{1}{2}$ pint (of ale).

GLUCOSE:
A directly fermentable sugar purchased in the form of "glucose chippings", large lumps, light brown in colour. Ferments well and imparts a little colour.

GOODS:
See **GRIST.**

GRAVITY
The density or weight of a liquid. (*See* Specific Gravity).

GREEN MALT:
Germinated barley before it is kilned.

GRIST:
The blended grain used with barley after it has been malted and crushed. Also called "Goods".

GRIT:
Any grain, other than barley, used in brewing. Raw and not prepared, like flakes.

GYPSUM:
Calcium sulphate or plaster of Paris. An important constituent of water ("or liquor") if beer is to clear well.

HARDNESS:
Quality in water desirable when brewing bitters or lights.
See **CALCIUM SULPHATE.**

HEAD:
The froth on beer. Good head retention is important, and is found in a well-conditioned beer with a good malt content, adequately hopped, since these factors contribute to its having sufficient surface tension.

HEADING LIQUID:
Used for adding an artificial "head".

HOP:
The flower of the hop plant (*humulus lupulus*) used in beer for its preservative and flavouring qualities.

HOP OIL:
A concentrate which can be used instead of dry hopping. It needs to be handled with care, for 1 drop is enough for up to 10 gallons. Hop oil gives the beer an added zest.

HYDROMETER:
Instrument for measuring the sugar content of a wort and strength of finished beer.

HYDROMETER JAR:
Jar in which hydrometer is floated for a reading to be taken.

INDIA PALE ALE:
See page 21.

INITIAL HEAT:
The temperature of the goods when the malt and hot water have just been mixed.

INVERT SUGAR:
Sugar which has been "inverted" by hydrolysis in the presence of acid. Often used in final stages of brewing, or for priming, since it ferments well.

INVERTASE:
An enzyme which breaks down sucrose into glucose and fructose, thus "inverting" it and making it fermentable.

IRISH MOSS:
A mixture of two marine algae, *chondrus crispus* and *Gigartina mamillosa*, used as a clarifying agent. It functions as a coagulant for complex and unstable proteins.

KILN:
Used in malting for drying malt after its germination.

KRAUSENING:
Adding some vigorously fermenting wort to another wort which has almost fermented out; a way of priming beer.

LACTOSE:
Milk sugar once used in Milk Stout. See page 47

LAGER:
See page 27

LEES:
See **BOTTOMS.**

LENGTH:
The volume to which the wort is diluted ready for fermenting.

LIGHT ALE:
See page 25

LIQUOR:
In brewing—water!

LITRE:
To a beer man ... $1\frac{3}{4}$ pints!

LONDON WATER:
Soft water, as found in London, and suitable for brown ales and stouts.

LUPULIN:
Yellow powder in the hop flower containing the oils and resins which give the hop its bitterness.

MALT:
Barley which has been so treated as to convert its starch into fermentable sugar.

MALT EXTRACT:
Malt wort concentrated into a syrup of honey-like consistency— a Godsend to the modern home brewer!

MALTOSE:
The fermentable sugar obtained by malting.

MASH:
Mixture of malt and hot water, or the combination of ingredients from which the beer will be made.

MASH TUB (or TUN):
Container for mash. A boiler or insulated container.

MILK STOUT:
Former name for a stout in which lactose (milk sugar) has been utilised.

NUTRIENT:
Nitrogenous matter added to wort to boost the action of the yeast; yeast food.

PALE ALE:
See page 25

PINT:
Imperial pint—20 liq. oz.; reputed pint—a 12 oz. bottle.

PITCH:
Add yeast to the wort to cause fermentation.

POLISHING:
Filtering beer through asbestos to give it brilliance.

POLYPIN:
See **EX-WINE FIVE.**

PORTER:
See page 26

PRIMING:

Adding a small quantity of sugar to a jar or bottle of beer to cause a slight further fermentation and give it a head and sparkle.

QUART:

A quarter-gallon.

RACK:

Siphon beer off the lees into fresh container: filling a cask.

ROUSE:

To stir or mix thoroughly, from bottom to top.

SPARGING:

Spraying the floating grains with hot water during mashing, whilst the wort is drawn off from below.

SPECIFIC GRAVITY:

The density or weight of a liquid compared specifically to that of water.

STOUT:

See page 26

TORRIFIED:

Roasted, as applied to malt.

TUN:

Name given to many vessels in a brewery (cf. Mash Tun). Once a measure (wine): 252 gallons.

ULLAGE:

The air space above the beer in a barrel.

WORT:

The liquid extract ready to be fermented.

YEAST:

The fermenting agent, in brewing usually a strain of *Saccharomyces cerevisiae*.

ZYMASE:

The enzymes responsible for fermentation.

CHAPTER 3

The Story of
Ale and Beer

What *is* ale or beer, and is there any difference?

It is perhaps only in this century that the two words "ale" and "beer" have come to mean almost the same. A more logical division of malt beverages today would be into "Beers" and "Stouts", hence the title of this book.

In this country today "ale" and "beer" are virtually synonymous; both denote a hopped, alcoholic drink made from malted barley, but this was not always so. Originally ale was malt liquor WITHOUT hops, and the term "beer" was not in general use in the modern sense until hops were introduced in the fifteenth century. Beer, or "beor", it is true, is mentioned in Anglo-Saxon writings, but it is not clear whether this was malt beer or a weak form of mead. And from A.D.950 onwards the word beor seems to drop from the language, only to reappear as "bere" or "biere" in the fifteenth century.

ALE

"Ale" is used differently in various districts and can denote almost any malt liquor except stout and porter.

Ale was often brewed specifically for certain important occasions or festivals of Old England. Thus, in rural life, there was **Lamb-ale,** for lambing time, **Cuckoo-ale**, for the day the first cuckoo was heard, **Leet-ale**, drunk in connection with the sitting of the old-time Courts Baron and Leet, **Harvest-ale** for the ingathering of the crops, **October-ale** and **Winter-ale** (aided and abetted, no doubt, by **Mulled Ale**). All in all, our forebears seem to have catered for most of the seasons. For university occasions there was **Audit Ale,** originally brewed at Trinity College, Cambridge, for audit day, and subsequently by other Oxford and Cambridge Colleges, **Brasenose Ale** and **College Ale.**

At one time much brewing was in the hands of the Church, which sold ale to raise money for special purposes, so that the word "ale" came also to be used to denote not only the actual drink, but also a special function or an occasion for fund-raising purposes— hence **Church-ale,** for a parish event, **Clerks-ale** for Easter, **Whitsun Ale**, and **Bride-ale**, the proceeds from the sale of which went to the bride. Similarly, there was **Bid-ale,** drunk at a party to which each guest brought a gift, and the reverse, **Give Ale,** a "free issue" bought as the result of a windfall or legacy.

ANCIENT ORIGINS

Ale and beer, it is true to say, have been brewed in one form or another for thousands of years, not only from malted barley but from maize and millet (in Africa) and rice (in Asia). Other grain has been and still is used either in place of barley or in addition to it.

Brewing is a craft which has its origins right back in the mists of antiquity. As long ago as 4000 B.C. beer was brewed in ancient Meso-potamia, where bread was mashed, malted and fermented, and the resultant brew flavoured with spices, dates or honey.

A thousand years or so later, legend has it, Isis, the mother of the gods, introduced it to the Egypt of the Pharaohs, where at least six types of beer are thought to have been in daily use. It was known as *Boozah* or *Hequp* and became the popular national beverage. It was probably from ancient Egypt that barley was first brought to Britain, so perhaps the word "booze" came with it! It was probably a "bitter", since it is believed to have been flavoured with rue, and cuneiform inscriptions giving detailed brewing instructions and quantities have been discovered by archaeologists. It is a whimsical thought that, 3,000 years before Christ, some now-forgotten Egyptian scribe set out to tackle exactly the same task as I do today.

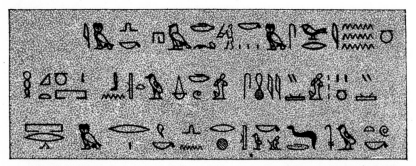

Note-pad reproduction of a dire warning contained in a 3,000 year old Egyptian book of etiquette. It reads: Don't boast about your drinking prowess. Two jugs of beer and even you cannot understand what you're saying. When you fall over nobody bothers to help you up. And your drinking companions, still upright, say "Away with this sot."

The Greeks certainly "had a word for it"—*Zythos*—and the Romans called beer *cerevisia*. In Spain the drink is called *cerveza* and in parts of France even today the old name for beer—*cervoise*—is still used instead of the modern *bière*, which derives from the German. *Cerevisia* stood originally for a weak mead, or honey beer, and the word is seen again in the Latin name for brewer's yeast—*saccharomyces cerevisiae*. Ceres was the goddess of the harvest of corn and we still see the same root word in "cereal." The Romans had beer as well as wine as an everyday drink, and rated it highly; Lucullus, the classic epicure, served it in golden goblets at his banquets and Julius Caesar gave it to his successful commanders.

Fermented drinks of one sort or another were being brewed in Britain before recorded history began, but they were probably meads made from the honey of wild bees, and it is not clear whether any malt liquors were made before the Roman invasion, but certainly during the 400 years of the Roman occupation ale was consumed in quantity in these islands, for in the Legions would be many recruited from elsewhere in Europe to whom beer was, like wine to others, one of the essentials of life. The Romans may thus have introduced the British to ale and the hop. Certainly the Britons, the Picts and the Scots all knew how to brew, and ale was served at their feasts and important celebrations.

When the Romans left, and the Saxons and Vikings descended upon Britain, brewing was one craft which persisted, for the Northmen were lovers of ale, quaffing it from drinking horns before battle and in their redoubtable feastings.

Ale houses became numerous, so much so that "Edgar the Peaceable", King of Wessex, had many of them closed, ordaining that there should be not more than one per village. At this period, too, drinking mugs were marked with pegs to define the size of a swig, and facilitate drinking contests! Hence our phrase about "taking someone down a peg . . ."

The Normans, too, were no strangers to malt liquor, and in the settled centuries after the Conquest brewing for the first time became feasible on a really large scale. Mostly it was the province of the monasteries and church, and the Domesday Book, for instance, records that the monks of St. Paul's Cathedral brewed 67,814 gallons of ale from 175 quarters each of wheat and barley and 708 quarters of oats. One cannot be exact because of variations in measures, but that

17

would be probably three times as strong as modern beers! Knowledge of brewing was even more widespread that it is today, and every housewife could turn her hand to it.

The first tax on ale (Henry II's impost on "movables") was levied in 1188 and from then on there were various enactments to control both quality and price, such as Henry III's Assize of Bread and Ale (1267) which tied the price of these commodities to those of grain and malt, and which lasted for three centuries. Heavy penalties were imposed upon bakers or brewers whose products did not come up to the mark in quantity or quality, so in the fourteenth century we find that well-known official, the ale-conner, or ale-taster, being introduced.

At this time there was, of course, no mechanical way of assessing a brew's worth so the ale-taster had authority to taste any brewer's ale, and order its price to be lowered if it was not satisfactory. The ale-conner (or al-konnere) wore leather breeches, and the practical test he employed was to pour some beer on a barrel end, and sit on it for a specified period. If, when he rose, his breeches stuck momentarily to the barrel, the beer was up to standard!

Incidentally, right up until local government reorganisation in 1973 my own borough of Andover had an official ale-taster who was solemnly appointed at Mayor-making each year, but he no longer took the oath of office and certainly did not wear leather breeches....

The Middle Ages were a great period of expansion and improvement in brewing. Ale was the national beverage, and honey the common sweetener, since sugar did not become popularly available until the middle of the eighteenth century. At first each ale house brewed its own, but gradually breweries sprang up, each supplying several houses, and in time these grew in size and importance. Much of the brewing was in the hands of the church, as already mentioned.

Brewing had become an accepted craft, and was given standing by Royal decree in 1406 when the Worshipful Company of Brewers—which still exists—was recognised as "the Mistery of Free Brewers"; in 1437 it was granted a charter by Henry VI to exercise control over "the brewing of any kind of malt liquor in the City and its suburbs for ever".

18

BEER

It was in the fourteenth century, too, that hops were introduced and the word "beer" reappeared. Hitherto Britain had drunk the fermented malt drink called "ale", but soldiers returning from the Hundred Years War (1338–1453) missed and demanded the drink to which they had become accustomed in northern France and Flanders, "*bere*" or "*bière*". This was an ale flavoured with hops, which then grew only on the Continent and not in Britain (where they were not planted before 1525). The Romans may have used them, but after their departure ale was flavoured in many ways with other herbs—nettles, rosemary, alecost (costmary) gruit (a mixture or herbs) or even ground ivy.

Like all innovations, the hop was bitterly opposed by the traditionalists, and there was fierce competition between ale-brewers and beer-brewers, the former bringing all possible pressures to bear against the use of the "wicked, pernicious weed." They managed to have legislation passed that only water, malt, and yeast could be used in the production of ale and it was not until 1493 that beer brewers were given craft recognition as a guild.

There were no indigenous hops in England, and the Kentish hop-fields were started in 1524–5 by immigrants from the Lowlands, which led to the suggestion in Sir Richard Baker's *Chronicles of the Kings of England* concerning 1524:

> *Tyrkeys, Carps, Hops, Piccarel and Beer,*
> *Came to England in one year.*

Once the hop *was* introduced (originally as a preservative), it grew more and more popular until it became eventually an essential part of the accepted flavour of beer. This process, however, took two or three centuries, and the old flavours persisted side by side with it. It is, as I have said, perhaps only in this century that "ale" and "beer" have finally come to mean the same.

The first Licensing Laws seem to have been introduced by Henry VII in 1495, and in 1552 Edward VI passed measures to control "taverns and tippling houses".

The Tudors—including Henry VIII—and the "first" Elizabethans—including Good Queen Bess—were all great beer drinkers (in those days one had beer for breakfast) and beer has, despite all its rivals, really remained the national favourite ever since. The seventeenth

Hogarth, William   **Gin Lane, c 1751**

century saw the introduction of fortified wines such as sherry and port, and of brandy, and since these were favoured by the "upper crust", beer tended to be less drunk at formal or official functions, though it remained the everyday drink of the nation.

It was a Stuart, Charles I, who imposed the first really effective taxation on beer in 1643, a trend that was continued by Charles II and his successors until nearly half the national income was derived from this source.

This went hand in hand with the development of brewing, which accelerated greatly in the eighteenth century. The middle of the century saw many still-famous breweries founded—Barclay, Bass, Charringtons, Coombe, Courage, Guinness, Meux, Simonds, Watney, Whitbread and Worthington, for instance—and brewing became truly big business, with a really impressive export trade.

This, of course, attracted yet more taxation on beer, malt and hops, and this in turn drove the people to drink cheap spirits, in England gin, in Scotland whisky; this was the dissolute period savagely lampooned by Hogarth in "Gin Row" and "The Rake's Progress".

In an effort to better conditions—and to improve the Government's popularity, then at low ebb—in 1830 taxes on beer were abolished, though those on malt and hops were retained. Licensing Laws were introduced in 1839, and have been constantly amended ever since. They still add some droll inconsistencies to the English way of life! The use of sugar in brewing was legalised in 1847.

The tax on hops was dropped in 1862 and the impact of science on the growing brewing industry made it possible for Mr. Gladstone in 1880 to abandon the tax on malt and introduce beer taxation based on specific gravity and the use of the hydrometer (or saccharometer).

At this time beers were strong, with gravities such as: strong ales 83–116; "Russian Stout" 116–131; porter 69–83; pale ale 55–69.

It was Mr. Gladstone's 1880 Act, incidentally, which applied to the home brewer, "the private brewer not for sale", a status which was determined by the rateable value of one's premises. Since this rateable value eventually became out of date and was not amended, the Act became meaningless, but it remained on the Statute Book, producing an incredibly complicated and unsatisfactory situation for would-be home brewers, right up until 1963, when Mr. Maudling removed all restrictions on home brewing.

MODERN BEERS

This century, of course, has seen the disappearance of hundreds of small breweries, and the emergence of mammoth brewery combines. This has meant the disappearance, therefore, of many once-popular and highly individual brews and a gradual flattening-out of variations in beers until only a few main types now survive. Draught beer once was king, and the most popular English beer was "mild" which could be drunk all evening without too much of a hangover, but as with all draught beer in wooden barrels its condition depended largely on the cellar work of the landlord. Today huge breweries bring science to their aid and more and more beer is artificially conditioned and the trend is steadily towards more and more "keg" beers. CAMRA, the Campaign for Real Ale, has in some measure reversed the trend by creating a demand for beer that has not been artificially carbonated, but it seems to me that they are trying to put the clock back and that modern keg beers, whilst they may not be so strong (because of taxation) are at least of consistent quality. Home brewers, however, can have both quality *and* strength!

Bottled beers, introduced just before World War I, have grown steadily in popularity, and in modern times canned beer sales have rocketed.

But by far the biggest change in the popularity stakes has been seen in lager sales, lager now bidding fair to displace bitter as the Britain's most popular drink, no doubt due to some consistently clever advertising and sales promotion in recent years.

Wadworth's Northgate Brewery, Devizes, Wiltshire, one of the few independent major breweries remaining

23

CHAPTER 4

Types of Beer and Stout

Nowadays it is perfectly possible to brew at home beers similar to most of the well-known named brands, and if you wish to carry your brewing knowledge that far and try experimenting on these lines it will pay you to read Dave Line's excellent "Brewing Beers Like Those You Buy" (AW Publications). But any brewer certainly needs to be able at least to recognise the principal types popular today, since they are the ones that appeal to the modern palate.

Ordinary ale or beer may be anywhere between 3% and 6% alcohol by volume, so that its average original gravity will have been about 30.

Other beers may be stronger, and therefore more expensive, since more malt will be used in their production and they may need longer storage.

Best Bitter: A general term for what is perhaps the highest expression of the brewer's craft, embracing Light Ale, Pale Ale, Indian Pale Ale and others of similar type, varying according to strength and hopping. All are straw-coloured, dry, with good bite, and are popular as bottled beers. Only the lightest and finest barleys, giving a pale malt, are used, and the relatively large amount of hops used gives a pronounced hop flavour, whence this beer, as draught, gets its description as "Bitter".

Light Ale: As its name implies, this is light in both colour (straw) and texture. Smooth, dry and well hopped, with a good "bite". Should be brilliant and have good head retention. Original gravity: About 30.

Pale Ale: Slightly more "body" than light ale, slightly more strength (O.G. anywhere between 40 and 45). Slightly more hops and slightly more colour (straw to light amber). India Pale Ale was originally specially brewed in the nineteenth century to be sent to our troops in India at the time of the British Raj; Burton Ale (no longer

25

necessarily brewed in Burton-on-Trent) has an O.G. of 45, bottled pale ales one of about 33. Pale ale should be high in malt bouquet, and well hopped, with a dry, fresh, clean taste.

Mild Ale: Varies enormously according to locality, but is usually less strong than bitter, darker in colour, less bitter (less hops) and slightly sweeter. Can be almost dark brown in colour. O.G. about 1030, alcohol 3–3½%. Once called **Four-Ale** (hence "Four-Ale Bar"). Now difficult to find.

Brown Ale: Can be similar to mild, but is usually slightly heavier and stronger (e.g. Newcastle Brown, Stock Ale, and Scotch Ale). Made from darker malts, kilned at higher temperatures and perhaps roasted. O.G.40.

Old Ale: Not quite so heavy or dark as most brown ales, but of high alcohol content and well matured. O.G.45.

Barley Wine: Very high in alcohol (O.G. about 80, that of a dry wine); colour preferably deep garnet; full, fruity bouquet, and an almost vinous flavour. Long maturation is necessary.

Stout: A peculiarly British drink, not brewed on the Continent. **Dry type:** As drunk in Ireland has about 5% alcohol, derived from an O.G. of about 45. It is very dark, almost black, and is made from much-roasted (or "torrified") barley, and the head is full and creamy. The bouquet is full and the taste sharply "woody" or bitter, as the result of high hopping and the use of roasted malts. **Sweet type:** Similar, but sweetened with caramel or lactose. **Milk Stout** is *not* made partly from milk, and the name has now been abandoned. It was so called because lactose, the type of sugar found in milk, is used in its manufacture. The blackest, strongest, and most popular **"Extra Stout"** is made from the most heavily roasted malts and is extremely difficult to imitate.

Porter was first made in 1722 (it was then known as "Entire") and became popular in the eighteenth and nineteenth centuries, and is so still in Ireland. It was a mixture of ale, beer, and "two-penny", a pale "small" beer. In appearance it is halfway between ale and stout and, as far as can be discovered, derives its name from the fact that it was the favourite tipple of market porters in London. (Porterhouse steaks were sold at the porter-house, the tavern where porter was sold). It is made with soft water and the original S.G. nowadays is about 40.

Lager, surprisingly enough, is quite difficult to make successfully, for it is not just a light, weak beer, as so many think, but the product of a rather different brewing system. British beers are produced by infusion and top fermentation, whereas **Lager,** the popular drink on the Continent and in America, is produced by decoction and bottom fermentation, with a slow secondary fermentation at a low temperature during the several months for which it is stored. In other words, it is a beer produced by a winemaking fermentation technique. The yeast employed is a special one, Saccharomyces Carlsbergensis, now available to the home brewer, and the hops are likewise usually special ones—Hallertauer or Saaz. The hopping rate is only about half that of beer. Colour should be straw (though there are *some* dark lagers to be found in Bavaria) and the lager should be lively, with good head retention. O.G.: about 1060. Taste: light, smooth, and clean, with plenty of malt and not too much hops.

Adding the hops to the boiling wort in open coppers in a smaller commercial brewery

CHAPTER 5

Background to Brewing

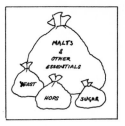

Brewing is basically a process of producing an alcoholic drink by the fermentation by yeast of a flavoured, sugary solution. When yeast, a living organism, is put into a solution containing sugar and certain other essentials, it "feeds" upon the sugar to obtain the energy it needs for self-reproduction, and a by-product of the reproductive process is the alcohol we seek.

As the yeast multiplies, it converts the sugar in the liquid half to alcohol and half to gas (carbon dioxide) by weight, the gas providing the sparkle and head so much admired in a good beer.

With beers the final alcoholic strength may be anywhere between 3% and about 6%. By increasing the sugar content we can increase the strength to 8% and even 10% so that the beer is really a "barley wine", but it should be noted that popular preference has always been for the weaker beers, since your beer drinker usually prefers quantity to strength.

In orthodox commercial brewing (as distinct from the making of simplified beers from kits, malt extract or ingredients other than barley) the basic material for providing the sugar is grain—in this country barley—which contains starch. Starch in its original state is not fermentable by the yeasts we wish to employ, so it has first to be converted to sugar, which *is* fermentable.

This is done by germinating the barley (malting) lightly milling it, and steeping it in hot water, or "liquor" (mashing). This sets up a chemical action which converts the starch in the malt to soluble carbohydrates, making sugar (maltose or dextrose) available for fermentation.

When studying the home production of beer, it is a great help to take a quick look at what happens in commercial brewing, for if we fully know the basic processes we are that much less liable to go wrong with our "home brew".

29

MALTING

After the barley has been cleaned, and all dust and "foreign bodies" removed, it has to be malted, or germinated. The grain is steeped in water for two or three days and, as it absorbs moisture, swells and softens. Surplus water is drained off and the grain is then malted, or germinated, in large drums which allow easy control of warmth and ventilation. The barley germinates and a tiny shoot, the acrospire, starts to grow within from the base of the grain and a gas, carbon dioxide, is given off.

Germination and growth may continue for about 10 days, at temperatures in the 13°–17° C. range, with plenty of aeration, by which time the acrospire, still within the husk, will be about three-quarters the length of the grain. Growth of this "green malt" has then to be terminated, and this is done by kilning, a drying process. Moderate heat is employed at first, 50°–70° C. (122°–158° F.) and then the temperature is raised to wither the shoot and, perhaps, lightly or heavily roast the malt. Final temperatures are lower for pale malts (80°–85° C.) than for dark malts (over 100° C.) and it is at this stage, by delicate variations of temperature, timing and method, that different flavours can be treated, and a whole range of pale, crystal, brown and black malts produced. The green malt may be kilned over wood chips, heated in an oven, or even roasted fully.

The kilning process is obviously a tricky one for the average home brewer, who dodges it by buying ready malted grain and thus starts with the next process which occurs in the brewery. . . .

CRACKING

The malt is then ground, or lightly crushed between rollers, and at this stage is known as "grist" (hence "grist to the mill").

MASHING

This, it must be emphasised, is the most important single operation in brewing, for it is here that the principal enzymatic change occurs in the malt. Enzymes are biological catalysts, or agencies within the grain which have power to change other substances without themselves being changed, and there are several which have all to play their part. The enzyme *cytase* dissolves the protective cellulose coating of the barley granules, giving access to the starch, which the enzyme *diastase* then liquefies and converts to fermentable sugar (or maltose), and dextrins which dissolve in the water to form a sweet, malt-flavoured liquid known as "sweet wort".

Enzyme activity is extremely sensitive to temperature changes, so by varying conditions during mashing the brewer is able to vary the wort and therefore the resultant beer. **The temperature in the mash tun must be between 62° and 68° C. (or 145°–155° F.).**

The grist is mixed with hot water in the mash tun, and other "grits" such as flaked barley, oats or maize may be added, and the temperature of 62°–68° C. is maintained for as least two hours. During this time the principal starch-to-sugar conversion takes place.

Then the sweet wort is run off from the bottom of the mash tun and at the same time the mash is sprayed (or "sparged") from above with hot water.

BOILING

The wort is then boiled with the hops at the rate of 1 lb.–5 lb. hops per barrel of 36 gallons (a) to stabilise the wort by sterilising it and preventing further enzyme activity; (b) to concentrate it to the required strength, and (c) to extract the preservative and flavouring qualities of the hops. Since some of these are volatile and would be driven off, it is usual to "dry hop", add some hops towards the end of this process. Boiling also assists eventual clarification by precipitating some of the complex malt proteins. From the boiler the wort is pumped to the "hop back", another vessel with a false bottom. The hops settle on to this and form a natural filter bed, through which the hopped wort drains on its way to the coolers and fermenting vessels.

FERMENTING

It is cooled down to about 15° C. (60° F.) and run into large fermenting vessels, and the yeast is "pitched". Top-fermenting yeast is used (except for lager) and the fermentation lasts about a week; when it is completed the beer is skimmed to remove top yeast, and racked into barrels.

CONDITIONING

The cloudy draught beer (cloudy because yeast is still in suspension in it) is then "fined", or rendered brilliant, by the use of isinglass, the flocculent fragments of which settle gradually, carrying down the suspended solids and leaving the beer above brilliant. Other conditioning, such as the addition of dry (unboiled) hops to pale ales, is practised to improve flavour and aroma, and to meet public taste. Treatment of the beer at this stage varies widely. Mild ales usually leave the brewery only a few days after they have been racked, and are often sweetened (or "primed"), but bottled beers and strong beers may be stored for weeks or months, during which there may be a slow secondary fermentation. Many home brewers puzzle over how to obtain a clear bottled beer with a good head, but without yeast deposit. The brewery overcomes the problem by fining the beer, chilling it, and saturating it with carbon dioxide under pressure.

Having seen what the commercial brewers do, let us see how we can adapt their methods for use in our home.

KEEP IT CLEAN

Make sure that all your equipment, fermenters, bottles, kegs and siphon tubes are really clean, and that your workplace is kept free of drips and splashes. Nothing grows a mould or breeds infection more quickly than spilt beer. Damp beer bottles are particularly dangerous and should be carefully inspected both inside and out, and stoppers, when re-used, should always be boiled or sterilised.

For simple cleaning of apparatus (as distinct from sterilising) one can use a solution of washing soda, 125 g (4 oz.) or of domestic bleach 25 g (1 fl. oz.) in 5 litres (1 gallon) of water.

For simple sterilising (as distinct from cleaning) one can use potassium metabisulphite. Make up a stock solution by dissolving 100 gm of the crystals in 1 litre of water (or 2 oz. in 1 pint). This gives a 10% solution which can be kept for convenience in a discarded plastic bottle previously used for washing-up liquid. When you want some solution for sterilising your equipment give a 2-second squirt from your bottle into 500 mls (or 1 pint) of water and it will be about right. Keep the squirter-bottle sealed when not in use.

Alternatively, dissolve 6 Campden tablets and $\frac{1}{2}$ oz. citric acid in 1 pint of water. Keep it in a stoppered bottle and avoid inhaling, since it is very pungent.

But my own way, being a lazy individual, is to combine both washing and sterilising, and this I do by using a proprietary powder, CHEMPRO, liberally. It cleans glassware, plastic and stainless steel magically in a few minutes and they afterwards require just a good rinse. This takes all the donkey work out of the business. VWP's cleaner/steriliser and STERAGLASS are similar excellent products.

For cleaning bottles, a regular job, I merely fill the sink with hot water and stir in two tablespoons of Chempro. Bottles are given a good soak—all stoppers are thrown in loose as well—and then well rinsed in plain water and drained in a rack before use.

Useful equipment for cleaning and sterilising bottles, jars and kegs – Chempro or VWP, or Campden tablets (sulphite) plus citric acid. Brushes of various shapes always come in handy, as do measuring spoons.

Washing bottles: care taken with this is essential to good brewing

CHAPTER 6

Some Important Points

"BALANCED" FORMULATIONS

Some important principles to remember in arriving at the formulation of any beer:—

1. The more malt, the more body, strength and head retention.
2. The more body, the more hops needed.
3. The more hops, the greater the bitterness and hop aroma.
4. The more sugar (household) the greater the strength but the thinner the beer if used instead of malt).
5. Never forget the importance of adequate boiling of the wort in producing quality beers.
6. The sooner bottled, the greater the risk!

STRENGTH

Now may I sound a warning?

DO NOT MAKE YOUR BEER TOO STRONG.

At first sight this may appear to be extraordinary advice. "Surely the whole point of brewing my own beer," you may well ask, "is that by so doing I can have a better beer than I can buy?" "Better", for most people, is at first synonymous with "stronger"

But strength is even less the principal criterion of a good beer than it is of a good wine.

After all, the extra strength is easy enough to achieve; one has merely to use more malt or sugar, and ferment for a longer period, and it is quite feasible to produce a beer, of, say, wine strength, up to 10–14% alcohol by volume.

But is it desirable? Breweries will tell you that their strongest beers are by no means the most popular, and the answer does not lie simply in the fact that they are more expensive. Until recent years the most popular beer in Britain was for a long time the weakest—mild, although today it has been supplanted by lager, itself not unduly strong.

Why is this? Surely the answer lies in the beer drinker's approach to his drinking. The beer drinker, unlike the wine lover, expects to be able to drink a fair quantity, say three or four pints, without ill effect; it should make his pleasantly relaxed, but not make him drunk, or leave him with a splitting headache the following day.

Any beer drinker who has had an "evening out" drinking a high gravity (i.e. strong, quality beer) will know what I mean! That is why your habitual beer drinker prefers the lower-gravity bitters and milds; he can drink them for a whole evening's darts without risk.

Surely the same is true of home brewed beer? It is neither wise nor hospitable to brew beer so strong that after two glasses your friend slips under the table or has a severe headache next day; he will not thank you for it! Home brewed beers are not a whit inferior to commercial ones, but they were once upon a time often made far too strong, with disastrous results upon host or guest, and it was this which earned them a quite undeserved bad reputation. Luckily the increasing use of kits is tending to correct this, since they produce beers of the proper strengths.

Aim at making your brews of roughly the same strength as the principal commercial types you are emulating and do not fall into the error of making them so *very* much too strong. If you *must* produce double-strength beer, or "barley wine", then please, please, treat it with respect, warn your friends of its strength, and serve it in smaller glasses, as publicans do their "nips" and "specials", and NOT in pint glasses or tankards.

YOU HAVE BEEN WARNED!

OBTAINING A HEAD

One of the principal difficulties which amateur brewers encounter with bottled beers is that of obtaining a good head, which does so much to make a home-brew look attractive. It is easy, by bottling prematurely, to produce a beer with a foaming, uncontrollable head, far more suitable for extinguishing fires than topping a tankard. It is also easy, by bottling too late, and adding no priming sugar, to produce a beer which is as strong as the sugar used allows, but flat.

The secret is to ferment the beer almost to completion (i.e. to a specific gravity of between 1005 and 1010), and then, when bottling, to add *just enough* priming sugar to produce a sparkle and head.

Usually this means a *level* teaspoon (5 ml) of sugar to a quart bottle.

One can also solve the problem by adding to a flat beer a "heading liquid" which can be purchased from suppliers, with full instructions, but this, while it gives an artificial head, does not seem to impart "life" to the beer, and is therefore not so satisfactory.

If head retention is poor it is probably the fault of poor quality malt (or using insufficient) or of not having allowed the beer to mature.

A magnificent head on a glass of homebrew

CHAPTER 7

Brewing from Kits

There are four main approaches to brewing at home, and they are (in order of simplicity, but not of quality or economy):—
1. A kit ("wet" or "dry").
2. Malt extract.
3. Mashing (using grain malt and other grits)
4. A combination of the second and third.

There is no doubt that the great majority of those taking up home brewing first do so by buying a proprietary beer kit, and this is certainly a wise way to start, since it is the ultimate in simplification.

There is an abundance of home brew kits available to enable one to produce a whole range of beers, many of them are really excellent . . . bitter, best bitter, stout, brown ale, lager . . . the lot! Over 80% of home brew sales consist of kits, and half the kits sold are for making lager.

Quality tends to vary according to price, as one would expect, but there is no denying that the leading kits give one beers that are every bit as good as commercial brands, and often both better and stronger, as an independent survey by "Which" revealed. They declared that the kits which produced the most *consistently* drinkable results were Boots, Cumbria, Karswood, Tom Caxton and Unican, whereas a Sunday Mirror survey in 1979 listed as "supreme home-brew bitters" Cumbria Special, Dakin's Bitter and Ceilidh Bitter, and as "Supreme home-brew lagers" Tom Caxton, Vina Can and Brew Riband. Almost all of them produce beer for between 6 and 8p a pint.

Most of the kits are very simple to use, since they consist principally of a 1.5 litre can of concentrated wort *which is already hopped*, and which makes 40 pints of beer. At one swoop, therefore, the processes of mashing and hop boiling are eliminated and the whole business of brewing is reduced to little more than adding water (some hot, some cold) and yeast, and then fermenting priming and bottling.

One or two "dry" kits are obtainable which employ malt or dried malt extract, with hops, and these make good beers but do involve longer boiling times.

The great advantage of the modern kit is that it streamlines your brewing and gives you a consistent, assured result. In almost all kits the instructions are simple and straightforward and obviously, which ever kit you buy, those are the ones to follow for the first few times. (Subsequently, as your experience grows, you may well be able to make minor adjustments to the formulation to suit your particular taste, e.g. by increasing or decreasing strength, by dry hopping, or by increasing or decreasing carbonation.)

EQUIPMENT

The other beauty of starting with a kit beer is that you need the minimum of gear, and can therefore try your hand at brewing with the least expense.

All you need is:
1. A 1 gallon (or larger) saucepan.
2. A brewbin (5–6 gallon).
3. A siphon tube.
4. A hydrometer.
5. 16 quart beer bottles and closures (or a plastic pressure barrel holding 5 gallons).
—all of which are described in detail in chapter 9.

Other small items such as scales, a large kitchen spoon, a funnel and a thermometer you probably already have in your kitchen. Some would argue that even a hydrometer is not strictly speaking necessary, but I think that for the small sum it costs it is invaluable to the beginner, for it tells him exactly when to bottle his beer, and thus enables him to avoid over-lively beer and burst bottles.

Kit beers differ only from extract or mash beers in the preliminary stages, i.e. in the preparation of the wort.

With most kits it is necessary to bring a few pints of water to the boil, and the hopped wort extract is then dissolved in the water and boiled for a short time; sometimes the addition of sugar is recommended so that a stronger beer is obtained, but beware of kits that advocate too little malt and a high proportion of sugar. The more malt and the less sugar the better the kit, as a rule!

The hot wort is then poured into the brewbin and made up to the correct length (usually 4 or 5 gallons) with warm or cold water, and is then allowed to cool, and from then on the brewing process is the same as for ordinary extract or mashed malt beers.

When the temperature has dropped to 24° C the yeast is introduced and the brewbin covered and stood in a warm place (18–22° C.).

Fermentation usually takes about 5 days, during which time the specific gravity of the wort (see: Hydrometer, p. 65) will attenuate from the initial 1035 or 1040 down to below 1010, and preferably to 1005.

The beer is then siphoned into bottles (or a plastic barrel) and priming sugar added at the rate of 1 *level* teaspoon (5 ml) per quart flagon, or $2\frac{1}{2}$ oz. per 5-gallon barrel. Instructions for various kits may differ slightly (some add finings) but this is the general procedure.

The beer is usually ready for drinking after a fortnight, but barrels take longer to clear since the yeast has further to fall.

MAKING A

Warming the extract to make pouring easier.
Stand the can in hot water

Pouring extract into the brew bin

Adding hot water and dissolving the extract

KIT BEER

Topping up to the desired quantity
(or "length") with cold water

Stirring thoroughly with a wooden paddle

Check the gravity of your "wort" with your
hydrometer; most beers have starting gravities
of 35–45°

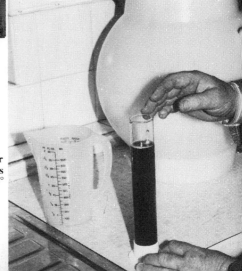

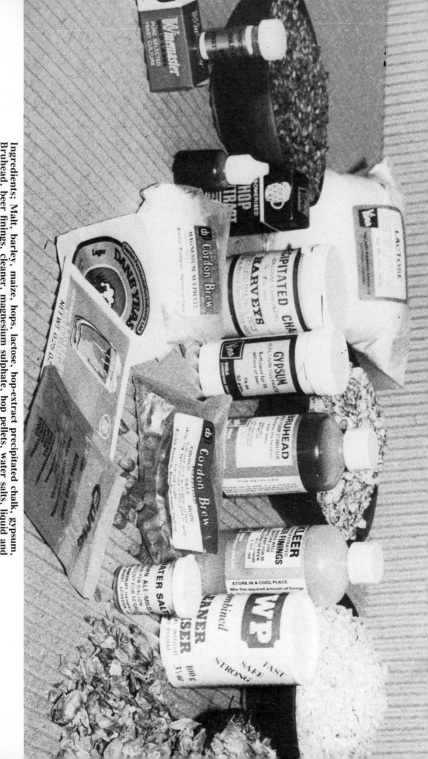

Ingredients: Malt, barley, maize, hops, lactose, hop-extract precipitated chalk, gypsum, Bruhead, beer finings, cleaner, magnesium sulphate, hop pellets, water salts, liquid and dried yeasts

44

CHAPTER 8

Brewing Ingredients

Having tried a beer kit you will probably soon wish to try your hand at formulating some of your own, thereby reducing expense still further. To do that you will need to know more about possible ingredients and equipment.

Principal ingredients, of course, are malt, hops, water and yeast (and, often added sugar and grains) so let us look at each in detail.

MALT

You *can*, if you wish, malt your own barley at home, and produce, say five or six pounds of malt, sufficient to make the same number of gallons of beer. Buy good, round-grained barley free of impurities, but before you go to the bother of malting all of it do a trial run to see if it will germinate. Take a few grains and soak them in water for 24 hours, then lay them between blotting paper in a warm place such as a propagator or a not too hot airing cupboard. They should sprout after a week or so.

If all goes well and the corn germinates, you can go ahead and malt the bulk, following the same procedure. Soak all the grain in some water in a plastic bucket at a temperature of 16°C (60°F) for 48 hours, changing the water four or five times. Then lay out the wet grain between damp newspapers, at a temperature of 16–18°C (60–65°F), and make sure it stays just damp, and does not dry out. After a week or so you should see the acrospire or growing shoot as a bulge half-way up the husk, which means that germination has been effected.

Put the grain on racks or trays in an oven with the door open and kiln or roast gently at 120°F for 12 hours. Turn the grains from time to time to achieve an even kilning. Do not overdo the process or enzymes in the malt which will be needed during mashing when brewing will be destroyed.

As will be seen, this is a rather fussy business, and most home brewers prefer to buy their malt, (ready malted barley) from a reliable home-brew supplier. It can be supplemented or reinforced by the use of malt extract, and other grits or grains (rice, maize, oats, rye etc). These can be employed to supply extra starch for conversion and make subtle flavour changes. An economy is to substitute sugar in one form or another for some of the malt, but this process must not be carried too far.

If one is formulating a recipe a sensible combination of malt, malt extract, grits, and sugar, is probably the most easy, economical, and satisfactory solution.

MALT QUALITY

Only the best barley goes for malting purposes, and once it has been malted, it should be thin-skinned and float when put into water, and it should still be sweet in taste and smell.

Some malts on offer are of poor quality, but a good malt on mashing, at 1 lb. to the gallon, could produce a gravity of up to 1025 (a brewery might get 25% more).

Malt, like coffee, can be roasted light or dark, and is sold under various descriptions and in various forms. But the main fact to remember is that the basic malt of all brewing, from which the strength of the beer is derived, is *pale malt*, **simply because this gives the highest yield.**

Generally speaking, the more a malt is roasted (i.e. the darker it is) the lower its yield. Thus pale malt is employed to obtain strength, coloured malts are added in small quantities to deepen colour or alter flavour.

Coloured malts are given various names, according to their depth of colour; thus one comes across crystal, amber, caramel, brown, black and "patent black" malts. **Crystal** and **caramel** malts will have been kilned in the same way as pale malt, but afterwards roasted lightly and are therefore a deep golden colour. They are excellent for adding "body" to sweeter beers. The content of the granule is crisp, and, used at 1 lb. per gallon, such a malt will give possibly 16 or 17 degrees of gravity, if mashing is carried out carefully. The yield is not so important as in the case of pale malt, of course, since these malts are likely to be used only to impart body or a more interesting colour to the beer, and need not be more than a twentieth of the total quantity of malt used; that is the commercial level. Used in large quantities, they can convey a very pleasant light and nutty flavour, as in the best bitter beers.

Amber and brown malts are similar, but slightly darker, and give a slightly deeper tone in the finished beer. The granule's contents are more powdery. These malts are useful for lending a smooth, full taste which is useful in the case of mild or brown ales. They are not used so much these days.

Black malt has been much more heavily roasted, at higher temperatures, so much so that it will give a wonderful depth of colour, but its yield in terms of gravity will be low, probably not more than two or three degrees per lb. per gallon. The roasting process is a delicate one, for if the temperature is too high the malt will be burnt, but if it is too low it will not be caramelised, and the temperature has therefore to be held between the two relevant levels (440°–480°F.). Black malts give stout its burnt and rather woody taste, and in the case of sweet stouts caramel is sometimes added to give the desired smoothness and sweetness. In a stout wort the alcoholic strength, again, is derived from pale malt, three parts of which will be used to each one part of black. **"Patent black"** malt is used in well-known "extra" stouts.

All these malts, of course, have to be mashed by the home brewer to extract the flavour, but he can take a short cut and avoid even this rather tricky job by employing malt extract. Generally, the principle to remember is: the more malt, the more the body imparted finally to the drink. And the more body it has, the more it will need some bitter herb added, to counteract the heaviness and keep the palate clear.

Roast Barley is not so rich in flavour as Black Malt and gives a drier finish, so is useful in, for instance, dry stouts. It is merely grain roasted to a reddish brown; it has not been malted.

ADJUNCTS

The starch in green malt is converted to sugar during mashing by the enzyme diastase. Diastase is sufficiently powerful to convert not only the starch of the malt, but that of any other grain (or "grit") that is added to it; a malt or malt extract which has this ability to a great degree is described as "highly diastatic". We can take advantage of this and reduce the cost—or increase the strength—of our brews by including in a formulation a proportion of other grits, such as flaked rice, flaked maize, flaked barley, or torrified barley, all of which must be cooled before use. Small quantities of these can be included in the boil-up when making extract beers, principally to effect flavour and colour changes, but also making a contribution to the beer's strength. They are described in more detail in "Mashed Beers."

There are other adjuncts such as torrified barley, wheat malt, wheat syrup and various brewing flours which are most interesting to experiment with, but they are not generally readily available. Oats and rye, too, are rarely used.

MALT EXTRACT

This the home brewer reconstitutes by the addition of water and hops, and the resultant wort can then be fermented like any other.

Some malt extracts are diastatic, so that other starch grits can be used with them, and their starch converted by the diastase of the extract. And some are already hopped.

SUGARS

In brewing the term "sugar" has a special meaning, for it covers anything which can be a source of sugar, or starch, whether malt, barley, maize, rice, or sugar-producing ingredient used in beer. Some of the sugar necessary in home brewing may come from malt (maltose), but sometimes it will be found too expensive to obtain in this way all the sugar necessary for a strong, or even a reasonably strong brew; consequently additional sugar will be needed. This can be added by means of ordinary white household sugar (sucrose), either cane or beet (chemically they are identical).

In Bavaria, incidentally, this is illegal, for German law recognises as beer only a drink made from malt, hops, and water; no other sugar must be employed. This has not been the case in breweries in this country since 1880 and the home brewer will certainly not wish to circumscribe himself in this way, when by adding extract or sugar he can make beer far stronger than that normally on sale.

As a rough guide to the total amount of sugar to be used, one can say most beers will require between $\frac{1}{2}$ lb. (250 gram) and 1 lb. (500 g) of malt, or malt extract, and possibly, in addition, up to $\frac{3}{4}$ lb. of sugar per gallon.

48

White Sugar

Relatively small additions of white household sugar or sucrose for the purposes of economy will not affect the flavour of your brew, but too much sugar, rather than extract or malt, will produce a thin but overstrong beer, poor head retention—and probably a hangover! The higher the proportion of maltose and the lower the proportion of sucrose, the better the brew, as regards flavour, body and head-retention. White household sugar is best for pale light-bodied beers.

Darker Sugars

Brown, moist sugars, on the other hand, are excellent for darker beers, giving a distinctive roundness and character to them, and are therefore well worth the extra cost when these special characteristics are needed. In this category fall Light Brown, Soft Brown, Barbados and Demerara sugars.

Invert sugar which is added to brewery wort before it is hopped and boiled, in order to increase its fermentability, undoubtedly ferments quickest of all, and can now be purchased. When yeast sets to work on sucrose, it first splits it into its two main components, glucose and fructose, or "inverts" it, making a sugar which is then speedily fermentable. Thus, by using invert, the fermentation is enabled to get away more speedily, since the yeast does not have first to effect the inversion.

If you use invert sugar (which is slightly more expensive than sucrose) note that since it contains more water it will be necessary to substitute $1\frac{1}{4}$ lb. for every 1 lb. of household sugar specified in recipes. It certainly makes a dry beer of real quality.

Invert sugar can be made quite easily as follows: Put 8 lb. ordinary sugar (sucrose, i.e. cane or beet) in a large pan with two pints of water and half a teaspoonful of citric or tartaric acid. Heat this mixture until it boils, stirring occasionally with a wooden spoon until the sugar has been dissolved. Boil gently for half an hour or so, cool, and add about two pints of water to give a total volume of exactly one gallon. One pint of this syrup contains one pound of invert sugar.

Glucose is now available to the home brewer and is an ideal material, for it ferments well and quickly. Best purchased in the form of honey-coloured *glucose chips* (lump form) which will impart both smoothness and a trace of colour to the beer, and at the same time produce a slightly drier beer.

Liquorice, a herb, is sweet to the taste, and can be useful for taking the harshness off a stout, but it should be avoided in finer beers, of which it will spoil the clean taste. It does give the illusion of added body and sweetness, plus a peculiar pungency of its own, but all it has in fact done is to coat the tongue.

Caramel, the commercial name for what used to be called *burnt sugar*, is most useful in brewing as a general colourant, and by its aid brews can be easily tinted from a light brown to a really dark colour, depending upon the quantity used. It can be purchased as liquid gravy browning, which sounds peculiar, but it will be seen from the label that this is in fact caramel. The amount to be used varies from a teaspoonful in three gallons for bitter to a tablespoon for a dark brown, and it is added at the boiling stage.

Caramel can be made thus: Put a dessertspoonful of white sugar into half a pint of water: bring to boiling. Do not stir. Lower gas or heat and let syrup simmer till it turns to white candy; then stir slowly. The syrup will gradually turn a light brown colour; keep stirring until the caramel is nearly black. Then remove from gas and put on approximately half a pint of cold water. Bring this slowly to the boil, stirring all the time until caramel is completely dissolved.

Lactose, the milk sugar that is added to what was once called "milk stout" (the name is no longer used nowadays, since it was held to be misleading, implying the inclusion of milk in the beer) is not fermentable by usual brewing yeasts, and therefore, if used, will remain in the drink simply as sweetening. It can be added to a stout, or other beer, at the rate of 3–4 ozs. to the gallon. Lactose can be purchased from most chemists, but one needs to be careful to buy only the best quality. If it has an unduly cheesy flavour, reject it. Generally speaking, its use as a sweetener is not recommended.

Artificial Sweeteners

Neither is the use of saccharin, which after a while breaks down and imparts a bitterness rather than a sweetness to the finished beer. Better for this purpose are sweeteners such as "Sweetex Liquid" or Sorbitol, used with great caution, a drop at a time.

Treacles and Syrups (Molasses, Black Treacle, Golden Syrup etc) are best reserved for experimental purposes, their flavours being so unpredictable; brown sugars are infinitely preferable.

It is the flowers of the hop that
we use in brewing

HOPS

The part which hops play in the production of quality beer is all important, for they affect both flavour, condition and keeping qualities.

The hop, with its delicate, fresh flavour (when used in small amounts) is the natural partner to malt: its bitterness, even when strong, is never disagreeable. Moreover, in an age of "tranquillisers", it should be recognised as a natural soporific (the "hop pillow" is an old remedy) and sleep comes easily after hopped beer.

The chemistry of the hop and its influence on the brew is complicated, but it is sufficient here to say that the hop contributes three main things: **volatile oils,** giving aroma and flavour; **resins**, giving bitterness and improving the keeping qualities of the beer, and **tannin-like constituents** which make for brilliance.

Originally, hops were regarded mainly as a preservative, but nowadays their flavouring function takes eminence, since the bitter flavour of hops has come to be appreciated and expected in a beer. The bitterness of a brew can be adjusted by increasing or decreasing the amount of hops used. The more hops, the more bitter the finished drink. High quality pale ales and bitter beers are heavily hopped, mild ales and stouts usually less so, and lagers least of all.

The degree of bitterness will also be governed by the *type* of hop chosen. Of the three constituents, oils, resins and tannins, it is one part of the resins, alpha acid, or humulon, which provides most of

51

the bitterness and keeping qualities. Beta acid is also present, and in larger quantities, but has only a tenth of the bittering power, so it has become the practice to grade hops by their alpha acid content, those with high alpha acid being generally the most sought after.

Generally speaking one-third to 1 oz. of hops (the dried cones which carry the seeds of the female hop plant, Humulus Lupulus) are used to the gallon, but exactly how much depends upon the type of hop and the type of beer being made. The higher the gravity the more hops will be required.

Thus light ale, mild ale and brown ale (all 30–35 SG) will require 0.4 oz. of hops per gallon, sweet stout and bitter (35–45 SG) will both need 0.5 oz., dry stout and pale ale (SG 40) 0.7 oz., and barley wine (SG 60) 1 oz. per gallon. Lager may require only $\frac{1}{4}$ oz. per gallon.

There is little point is giving an exhaustive catalogue of hop varieties, since they will not all be generally available to the home brewer, so I list here only popular and widely used varieties. It may well be that even these will eventually be unavailable owing to the impact of mechanical picking and E.E.C. regulations. Harvesting by machine demands sturdy vines, and our native Golding and Fuggles, for instance, do not stand up to this, so are gradually being replaced. And the Continent insists upon seedless hops, whereas the British ones are allowed to set seeds. So the E.E.C. poses an obvious threat to British hops. Generally speaking, more hops are employed in British beers than in Continental ones.

Most of the following are available:

Fuggle: (alpha acid 3.5–4.2%) A Kentish hop which has been used for over one hundred years, and which is probably still the favourite of the brewing industry. Strong-flavoured, and therefore useful in the stronger-flavoured beers such as mild and brown ales. *W.V.Gs* (4.5%–5%) and *Bramling Cross* (5–6%) are similar.

Golding: (3.5–5%) Named after a Kentish grower who established the strain over 160 years ago, this hop is lighter in flavour, and is best used in light ales, best bitters, and beers of that type. Excellent for dry hopping if so desired.

Northern Brewer: (6–8%) A markedly bitter hop, so much so that 2 oz. is enough for $4\frac{1}{2}$ or 5 gallons: excellent in stouts.

Bullion (alpha acid 4–9%) An American variety noted for its outstanding bitterness. Its strength of flavour is such that it can really only be used in conjunction with other hops, but is particularly valuable in stouts, or particularly bitter beers, and in beers which are to have a long maturation period.

Hallertauer: (7–9%) A Bavarian hop which is now being imported and from which noble beers can be brewed. Particularly useful in light, grain malt beers.

Saaz: (6–8%) Another imported hop which is ideal for the making of lager, since it has a delicate, dry flavour and not too pronounced an aroma.

Many brewers are tempted to try harvesting and drying wild hops, which are often to be found in the countryside, but this is usually an abortive exercise. Their inferiority and the impossibility of proper control during the drying process produces a poor quality dried hop, and that in turn means a low-grade beer. Do not be tempted, for the same reason, to buy cheap, old compressed hops which have probably lost most of their aroma.

Styrian Goldings: (6–8.5%) despite their name, are more like Fuggles in their characteristics. Very expensive.

Other varieties which may be encountered and occasionally purchased include: Bramling, Brewer's Favourite, Brewer's Gold, College Cluster, Concord, Copper Hop, Defender, Density, Early Bird, Early Choice, Malling, Midseason, OF/27, Pride of Kent, Quality and Sun Shine.

HOP PELLETS AND POWDERS

It is useful to have such background knowledge about hops, and any keen brewer will profit by reading Dave Line's "Big Book of Brewing" or Wilf Newsom's "The Happy Brewer", which both go into the subject in more detail.

It seems likely, however, that the use of whole hops may gradually become a thing of the past for in the commercial world they are rapidly giving way to hop pellets, or processed hops in other forms. These have now been introduced into the home brew trade, which will undoubtedly be trying to persuade their customers to use them because of their smaller volume and general convenience. The only snag is that they do not provide a natural filter bed like the whole hop, and can lead to cloudy beers unless used with care, and they are probably best employed in conjunction with ordinary hops. The pellets and powders such as Hopstabil are sold in sterile, sealed sachets to protect their flavour and maximise their keeping qualities, and are well worth experimenting with, since they offer a quick road to good flavour.

Isomerised Hop Extracts are sold under various trade names such as "Hopcon", and are highly concentrated extracts of the essential hop oils and resins, obtainable in two or three strengths. They can be used to add additional flavour and aroma to a finished beer, and are very efficient indeed employed in this way, but owing to their extremely high concentration must be used with the utmost caution; a drop of the oil to a gallon is often sufficient. It is best added to a jugful of the beer before bottling and then stirred well in, the jugful then being returned to the bulk and well stirred.

OTHER HERBS

Although the hop is now pre-eminent, other herbs can be used to impart both flavour and bitterness, and for centuries were, and it is well worth-while to experiment with them. Spruce oil, for instance. It is also a good preservative (and combines well with hops) but, unlike hops, will dispel drowsiness rather than create it. Consequently, spruce beer, with its clean fresh flavour is a good refresher. It is still popular in Scandinavia. Nettles were once used in making stouts. An infusion of nettle is slightly salty (a requirement in stouts) and if nettle is used it will need plenty of hops or the roughness of black malt to give it an edge and make it palatable. Salt gives beer, like coffee, a "roundness" of flavour, but as soon as the salty taste becomes perceptible it is unpleasant, and the characteristic clean after-taste of beer is lost. Other old-time flavourings were ginger, dandelion, burdock or sarsaparilla, and one can experiment with these—to find stimulating variations upon the more usual hop theme. Once the principle of balancing sweetness against bitterness is understood it becomes easy. It is worth trying some of these flavourings experimentally, if only to see just why the hop eventually won!

WATER (OR LIQUOR)

It is not accidental that the best beers in Britain are brewed at Burton-on-Trent, that Hampshire is famous for its bitter, or that Ireland, like London, is renowned for her stouts and porters, for the brewing of particular beers was once very much a matter of the composition of the water in the locality. High quality pale ales and bitter beers such as produced at Burton-on-Trent demand the type of water which occurs there naturally, water containing a comparatively high proportion of gypsum, or calcium sulphate. This helps one to attain clarity in the finished beer because it aids the separation of certain nitrogenous elements in the malt, which can be filtered off with the spent hops.

It has been said that to be ideal for bitters such water should contain 21 grains per gallon of calcium sulphate and 7 grains per gallon of magnesium sulphate. Chlorides are not essential.

Mild ales and stouts and the best lagers, on the other hand, are made with soft water, often described as "London type", containing a fair amount of calcium and magnesium carbonate and a certain amount of chlorides.

Generally, it will pay you to make the type of drink best made with your local water, soft or hard, and to ignore the niceties of water adjustment. Certainly that is the best plan if you are making kit beers. Far more important is to keep an eye on the quality of your water supply and, for instance, to avoid brewing on any occasion that it is noticeably chlorinated. If, however, you wish to progress to the real niceties of brewing it will pay you to study "Water Treatment" in Chapter 10.

YEAST

Baker's yeast is not satisfactory for beer because it does not settle down into a firm sediment and will rise in clouds in the beer at the slightest movement of a barrel or bottle or when a screw stopper is removed. Racking is difficult and undue wastage is caused.

Most breweries have their own favourite strains of *saccharomyces cerevisiae*, which do have some effect upon the character of their finished products, and if you are lucky you can sometimes obtain a jar from your local brewery. Such a yeast is naturally excellent for your purpose, for it will aready have a pronounced beery flavour, and once you have some, if you are brewing weekly, you will always have an ample supply, and probably an almost embarrassing surplus. I once kept one such brewery yeast continually in use for over two years. At that time I was brewing weekly in glass jars and all that was necessary, after racking one brew into half gallon bottles, was to throw out two-thirds of the lees, leaving just sufficient to fill the peripheral groove at the bottom of the jar. The new wort was then siphoned in on top of this and fermentation would begin immediately.

There is always an active yeast sediment in "real ale", so if you are on sufficiently good terms with the landlord at your "local" he may be persuaded to let you have half a pint or so from the bottom of a cask for you to culture onwards.

You can also make a starter bottle from the dregs of a bottle of certain bottled beers! Allow the bottle to stand undisturbed for two or three days, then pour off your drinks leaving a couple of inches of beer behind, containing any yeast which may be in that particular bottle. Make up a solution of $\frac{1}{4}$ pint of hot water, 1 teaspoon of sugar, 1 teaspoon of malt extract and a lump of citric acid the size of a pea and, when it is cool, pour it into the beer bottle, plug it with cotton wool and stand it in a warm place, such as the airing cupboard. If you are lucky (it depends largely on what type of beer or stout you are using) you will get a vigorous fermentation which can be used as a starter for your next brew. Several of the better known bottled beers can be used in this way. Guinness is excellent and one which is rarely found to fail is Worthington White Label. The dregs of a bottle of home brew, of course, make an excellent starter for a following brew, because there is much more yeast sediment in a bottle of home brew than in a bottle of commercial beer. So once you have acquired a tiny amount of true brewer's yeast you need never be without ample supplies, indeed you are eventually likely to have so much that you will be throwing quantities away every time you bottle.

Brewery yeasts, it should be noted, are usually top fermenting varieties, and this often involves some skimming, for a thick "cake" of yeast will form and float on the surface of the beer. I find that the particular top yeast which I most commonly use produces a real mat of yeast on the surface of the beer, so much so that skimming is necessary every two days or so.

The initial scum and surplus yeast should be skimmed off, but once a creamy foam appears—the so-called "cauliflower head" or "rocky head", do not skim again until you are going to bottle. A few teaspoons of yeast from the lees of a brew can also be used.

Such surplus yeast, of course, provides an excellent starter for the next brew, but there is always far too much, and quantities have to be thrown away.

Yeast will keep about a week in the wet state. Take a few spoonfuls from the pancake of floating yeast, or from the lees, and dry them off on clean blotting paper or cloth. Then mould the yeast into a knob, put it into a polythene bag or glass jar with loose-fitting lid, and pop it into the 'fridge until wanted.

Most brewers, we feel, will at first plump for a reliable granular yeast such as is sold by home brew shops in sachets or tubs and which are quite satisfactory, if not quite as good as a wet yeast from a brewery. Use about a level teaspoon to the gallon.

Lager yeasts (which are bottom fermenters and not top fermenters) are excellent, but more expensive. They do settle firmly, allowing the clear beer to be racked off easily.

There is little point is using a nutrient with the yeast as one does in winemaking, for malt extract is itself a superb nutrient, but in cases of sluggish fermentations or where fermentation is slow to start it may be useful to add a proprietary yeast energiser and/or a good pinch of citric acid to a 5-gallon brew. That is enough to give the trace of acidity which yeast likes, without affecting the flavour.

Scum and surplus yeast should be skimmed off: use a flour sieve

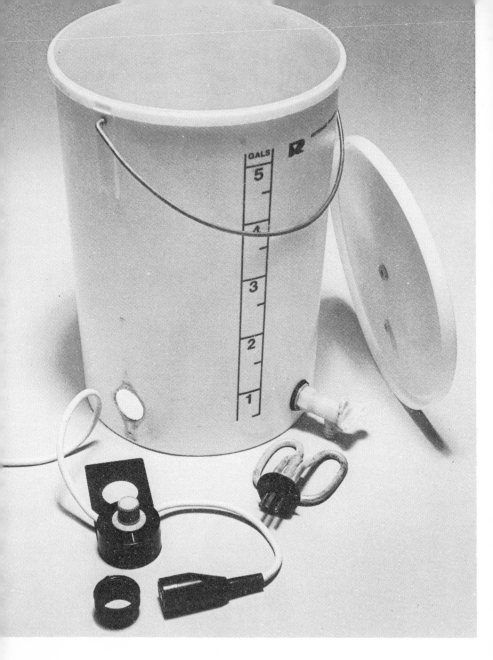

A Bruheat boiler dismantled for cleaning

CHAPTER 9

Equipment you will need

Since beer, obviously, is drunk in larger quantities than wine, by the pint or half-pint, one naturally tends to brew in greater bulk, and, whilst once can still make experimental single gallons, most home brewers eventually come round to the idea of making four or five gallons at a time. This is about the largest quantity that a man can comfortably lift; ladies may have to be content with $2\frac{1}{2}$ or 3 gallons!

BOILING

Most *kit* beers do not demand the use of a large boiler and you may well be able to manage with a large $1\frac{1}{2}$ or 2-gallon saucepan in which to boil sufficient water to dissolve the extract, adding the remainder cold.

It will not be long, however, before you start thinking of equipment yourself to brew in rather more sophisticated fashion, and if you intend attempting mashed beers you will certainly need to do so, since you will need to be able to boil and handle larger quantities.

If you have a larger boiler to sit on a gas stove, such as a four or five-gallon aluminium one, or even a 3-gallon "dixie" such as I used for some years, you will find it useful, but there is no doubt that in the long run the ideal solution is an electric or gas boiler holding about seven gallons. It is certainly necessary if you are making beers other than from kits. I use a purpose-designed BRUHEAT boiler which is perfect for the job, and which can be obtained from home-brew shops. It is a large polypropylene bucket fitted with an electric element, controlled by a sensitive thermostat that has a range between 10°C and 100°C and thus can cope with all three processes involved, mashing, boiling and fermenting.

Iron or galvanised boilers, incidentally, are safe enough for water or for boiling up a mash, but should not be used if any acid whatsoever is in the formulation, since there may be a risk of metal poisoning.

BAG FOR INFUSING

For infusing hops a large bag of nylon mesh, with a string for easy removal, is useful. The hops can be boiled in this and are easily removed before fermenting begins. You can either make a bag yourself or buy one at a home brew shop.

FOR MASHING

When making a beer or stout from malt or other grain there are two main methods you can follow. You can mash the grain in a large saucepan, or in a polythene bucket with immersion heater, and then sparge into your boiler, straining the grain in a stout bag with a mesh bottom inside your boiler. Or you can mash in the bag in the Bruheat boiler, using part of your wort.

If you use a 2-gallon polythene bucket you will also need a 50-watt immersion heater, with or without thermostat. And a thermometer (5° to boiling point) is indispensable.

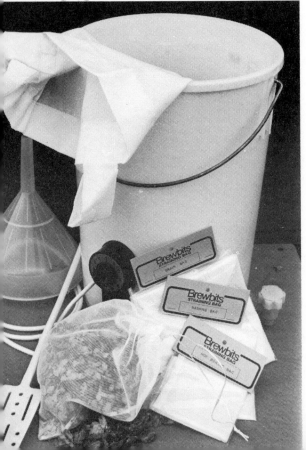

A Bruheat boiler, various useful bags, polypropylene stirrer and funnel

FOR FERMENTING

For fermenting and general brewing uses the best buy is undoubtedly a white plastic "brewbin" holding about six gallons, to be obtained from home brew shops, Boots or Woolworths. Made of food grade white polystyrene, such bins are safe, light, easy-to-clean and a joy to use, and they have an airtight lid to which a fermentation lock can be fitted if desired. They cost only about £2.50, and are virtually essential. It is particularly helpful if your bin is graduated in gallons and litres either inside or out, and if it is translucent so that you can see how much it contains. This is useful when handling large quantities of liquid.

An alternative is a plastic dustbin, but if it is coloured it will need to be lined with an uncoloured polythene bag, since the colourants and plasticisers in non-food grade bins can be toxic. An even cheaper solution is to use such a plastic bag inside the cardboard "outer" of a 5-gallon ex-bulk-sherry container, which are often obtainable for the asking at wine shops and off licences.

Whichever you use, this becomes your primary fermenter.

A range of fermentation bins, 2½–5½ gallons

FOR MEASURING

Do not fiddle about in beer brewing with 1-pint measures. A 1-gallon glass jar or saucepan will save a lot of time, as will marking out quantities on your brewbin. But make sure that your jar *does* hold 8 pints, (some hold more, some less) and then reserve it for that purpose.

FOR STRAINING

Straining of small quantities is best done with a large nylon flour sieve, easy to use and clean, but if you are dealing regularly with big quantities of hops, and grain or bran, it will pay you to make a wooden "picture-frame" crisscrossed by tape or cord, to fit the top of your vessel. Or use a garden sieve. On this it is then a simple plan to lay a piece of muslin, and the whole mash can be tipped out in one go and left to drain, instead of having to be strained a little at a time.

FOR SIPHONING

Make yourself a siphon from five or six feet of transparent acrylic tubing. You can either fit it with a glass or stainless steel J-tube at the intake end (so that it draws clear beer down from above and does not suck up sediment) or fit it with a float as illustrated. Use a thick 8 in.

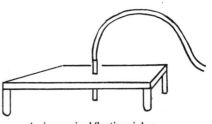

An improvised floating siphon

disc or square of wood and push the end of the tube through a hole in the middle so that it projects slightly underneath. Some 1 in. dowel legs glued and screwed underneath prevent any great disturbance or pickup of sediment.

FOR "RESTING" YOUR BEER

To keep expense to the minimum, pay a visit to your local wine-merchant, grocer or off-licence and beg one, or better still two!, of those flexible plastic cubes with a non-drip tap and in a cardboard outer. These polypins are used for draught sherries and wines, and since they are non-returnable, can usually be had for nothing, or the price of a pint. (One outer can be used to contain a plastic bag as your primary fermenter, if you wish). They are very handy for "resting" your beer for a week or so before bottling or barreling. But keep the tap open and fit an improvised air lock to it.

FOR EASY HANDLING

Make yourself a trolley from a rectangle of ½-inch wood—I used marine ply—with a strong castor fixed under each corner, so that it stands 2 or 3 inches high. Your dustbin, or primary fermenter stands on this and the wort can easily be run into it from your boiler's tap. Such a trolley makes it possible to move a 5-gallon (or even bigger) brew with ease.

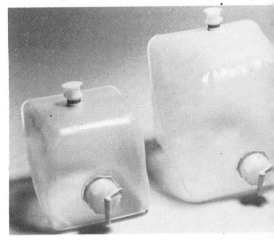

The two and five gallon polypins on the market today

A trolley like this takes away a lot of the hard work

FOR WATER IN QUANTITY

I have also found it extremely useful when handling these large containers (which are too big to fit under the tap in many kitchen sinks) to have a four-feet domestic hose which fits on to the mixer tap and which has a rigid piece of tubing to give a smooth jet at the delivery end. This makes washing out, rinsing and filling of large containers with either hot or cold water much easier.

FOR BOTTLING

For bottling your beer you will need to collect or buy beer or cider flagons of thick strong glass, capable of withstanding the 30 lb. p.s.i. pressure that will be generated inside them. Wine bottles, spirit bottles and any bottle not designed to stand up to such pressure are lethal.

You will need 16 or 20, since you will probably be making beer four or five gallons at a time. You can either retain them when you buy bottled beer or purchase a couple of dozen outright at an off-licence, public house, or home brew shop. Reject any which are cracked, or which have chips around the neck or base, making the bottle weak at that point and leading to a risk of its exploding as pressure builds up within it.

Nowadays you are most likely to come across bottles which have to be sealed by special tin crown caps. These can be obtained quite cheaply from home brew shops and are easily crimped on to the bottles by a simple tool, giving your bottle a truly professional air. One can also buy push-in plastic closures such as continentals use for wine bottles and some breweries now use to re-seal crown-closed bottles.

Two handed capper, mallet, knock-on capper, and various closures

You may be fortunate enough still to come across some of the screw-stoppered flagons which were once in common use: if so, grab them, because although they are perfect for our purpose, they are fast becoming obsolete. They are economic to use because the stoppers can be sterilised and used over and again. Check that the rubber rings are not perished or missing; if they are your beer will go flat. If any show defects, obtain replacements.

FOR BOTTLE-CLEANING

Wire-handled bottle-cleaning brushes are useful for an even more handy idea is a cube cut from a nylon scouring pad and fixed with glue or wire to the end of an 18 in. dowel.

FOR CHECKING GRAVITY—THE HYDROMETER

The hydrometer, like the thermometer, will enable you to brew with precision.

The *beer* hydrometer (usually graduated 1000–1100) will tell you the gravity of your wort, the strength of your beer, and, most importantly, when it is safe to bottle. Most beers have starting gravities between 1010 and 1060, as will be seen from this table, and must on no account be bottled if the final gravity is above 1010.

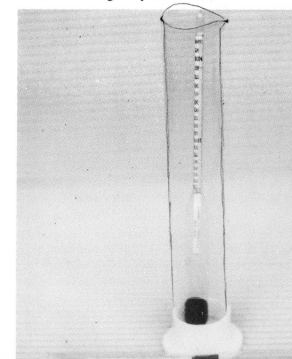

Hydrometer and jar

Typical starting gravities of commercial beers are: (Sugar in the table below, means sugar and/or malt):

Type of Brew	·S.G.	Potential % alcohol by vol.	Amount of sugar in the gallon lb. oz.		Amount of sugar added to the gallon lb. oz.		Vol. of one gallon with sugar added gal. fl. oz.	
	1010	0.9		2		2½	1	1
	1015	1.6		4		5	1	3
	1020	2.3		7		8	1	5
	1025	3.0		9		10	1	7
Mild, light, lager	1030	3.7		12		13	1	8
Pale ale, bottled	1035	4.4		15	1	0	1	10
Pale ale, porter	1040	5.1	1	1	1	2	1	11
Strong ales, stout	1045	5.8	1	3	1	4	1	13
,, ,, ,,	1050	6.5	1	5	1	7	1	14
"Extra" stout	1055	7.2	1	7	1	9	1	16
Very strong ales	1060	7.8	1	9	1	11	1	17
,, ,, ,,	1065	8.6	1	11	1	14	1	19
,, ,, ,,	1070	9.2	1	13	2	1	1	20

Subtract the final gravity from the initial gravity and divide the answer by 7.36 and that is the strength of your beer in terms of percentage alcohol by volume.

It is interesting to compare the strengths in tne third column above with those of other drinks, e.g.: Claret 9.7%, Chateauneuf du Pape 12.5%, Champagne 13.5%, sherry 18.9%, port 20.2% and whisky 40%.

Do not forget that hydrometers are designed to be read when the liquid is at 59°F., and if it is at any other temperature you should allow for it as in the following table. Omit the "decimal point" of the specific gravity and make the correction to the last of its four figures.

Example: A hydrometer reading of 1140 at 86°F. should be corrected to 1143.4.

Temperature		Correction
°C.	°F.	
10	50	Subtract 0.6
15	59	Correct
20	68	Add 0.9
25	77	Add 2
30	86	Add 3.4
35	95	Add 5
40	104	Add 6.8

A typical record of the progress of a fermentation:

Initial S.G. of wort before adding yeast				...	...	...		1040
S.G. after 1 days ...	...	...	...	...	...	...		1034
,, ,, 2 days ...	...	...	...	...	...	...		1023
,, ,, 3 days ...	...	...	...	...	...	...		1011
,, ,, 4 days ...	...	...	...	...	...	...		1006
,, ,, 5 days ...	...	...	...	...	...	...		1003
,, ,, 6 days ...	...	...	...	...	...	...		1001
,, ,, 7 days ...	...	...	...	...	...	...		1000

OTHER USEFUL EQUIPMENT

From this you will see that a highly efficient set-up capable of regularly brewing 5 gallons at a time would include:

Bruheat or other large boiler.

6-gallon brewbin, with lid.

One or two 4½–5 gallon polypins.

Siphon.

Beer hydrometer and jar.

Thermometer (0–100°C).

5-gallon pressure barrel, preferably with injector,
 OR

24 quart beer bottles.

A large wooden spoon or paddle.

In addition to this you will need things probably already in the kitchen ... scales, measures, kitchen spoons, a 5 ml. measuring spoon, a large sieve or strainer, and, if bottling, a bottle brush, a small funnel, crown caps, and a capping tool.

Your home brewery is now well equipped and ready to go into production!

CHAPTER 10

Brewing Techniques

Whichever way you are making your beer certain essential processes are likely to be involved, such as

a) Adjusting the water quality, if necessary.
b) Boiling the wort.
c) Fermenting.
d) Racking off and "resting".
e) Fining.
f) Bottling or barrelling.
g) Carbonating.

WATER TREATMENT

Water treatment for brewing purposes is a complicated subject, and if you wish to go in for competitive brewing it would be as well to study it further. Most home brewers, however, will find it sufficient just to ascertain from their local Water Board the exact composition of their own supply.

This is a terrifyingly detailed document but the only factor with which you need concern yourself is the TOTAL hardness. (Hardness is sub-divided into "temporary" and "permanent", temporary hardness being that which is removed by boiling. Total hardness is sometimes given in parts per million (milligrams per litre) and sometimes as Clarke's Degrees, and waters are classified, using these scales, as follows:

TOTAL HARDNESS		WATER TYPE
p.p.m. *mgm/litre*	*Clarke's* *Degrees*	
0–100	0–7	Soft
100–200	7–14	Medium Soft
200–400	14–28	Moderately Hard
400–600	28–42	Hard
Over 600	Over 42	Very Hard

It is sufficient for our purpose to distinguish between soft and hard. You probably know quite well which your water is, but if you do not, just boil a gallon of water for twenty minutes or so, let it cool, and see if it leaves a chalk deposit; if it does the water is hard. Those who have lived in a hard water district will recognise this phenomenon in their kettles!

Once you know whether your water is hard or soft you can easily adjust it for various brews.

Use a 5 ml. medicinal teaspoon as measure. I have used the common name of the substances but if you have to order them from a chemist they are: Gypsum—calcium sulphate; Epsom Salts (magnesium sulphate), chalk (calcium carbonate) and salt (sodium chloride). adjust as follows:

TREATMENT FOR FIVE GALLONS OF WATER

HARD

Bitter, Light and Pale Ales, Strong Ale, Barley Wine.	Add 1 teaspoon flaked calcium chloride OR: boil for $\frac{1}{4}$ hour; siphon off, Add 1 teaspoon gypsum and $\frac{1}{2}$ teaspoon Epsom salts.
Mild Ale, Brown Ale, Stout (sweet)	Add 1 teaspoon flaked calcium chloride OR: boil for $\frac{1}{4}$ hour; cool; siphon off. Add $\frac{1}{2}$ teaspoon salt.
Irish stout (dry)	No treatment required.
Lager	Add 1 teaspoon flaked calcium chloride OR: boil for $\frac{1}{4}$ hour; cool; siphon off.

SOFT

Bitter, Light and Pale Ales, Strong Ale, Barley Wine	Add 1 teaspoon gypsum and $\frac{1}{2}$ teaspoon Epsom salts.
Mild Ale, Brown Ale,	Add $\frac{1}{2}$ teaspoon salt
Stout (sweet)	Add $\frac{1}{2}$ teaspoon salt.
"Irish Stout"	Add 1 teaspoon precipitated chalk.
Lager	No treatment required.

You can purchase in home brew shops "water treatments" for different types of beer; you simply need to make sure that you have the right one for your water and for the beer you intend making. Lobbing in a "water treatment" without knowing what it is or what it will do is not much help!

BOILING

. . . is necessary for several reasons, but principally to ensure that the wort is sterilised, to extract flavour from any loose hops employed, and, particularly with mashed beers, to achieve a "hot break", or clarification by causing the flocculation of protein matter in suspension.

In the case of grain beers and mashed beers the wort must be boiled for at least threequarters of an hour, and preferably threequarters more in order to achieve this "hot break". And it is not sufficient just to simmer; it must be a good rolling boil. Eventually the beer will clear, and if a glassful is removed it will be seen that the proteins in suspension are clumping together in little lumps about the size of a match-head, and settling. When this occurs you have achieved the hot break but if when you test the solids are still minute and in cloudy suspension more boiling is necessary. Irish Moss may be added during the last quarter of an hour to speed the process.

A point to note is that boiling also progressively darkens the wort, and therefore the finished beer. Half an hour will give a pale beer, but less will give an anaemic looking one (quite apart from the fact that the wort will not be stabilised. Up to $1\frac{1}{2}$ hours will produce a proportionately darker beer. For stout and extra stout, of course, black malt should be used to achieve that depth of colour.

Some recipes reduce the boiling period to a minimum (this is obviously an attraction to the beginner) but it is really a mistake, and it is preferable if the smell and steam from your "brewery" cause objections from the distaff side, to use an electric boiler on an extension lead in the garage, or even outdoors.

Ample boiling time is important if you are to obtain beers of quality, you will find.

Sterilisation is achieved quite rapidly, but it is important to allow sufficient time for the full extraction of the flavour and aroma of any hops used, and this usually means at least three-quarters of an hour. So for most beers, on all counts, hop flavour extraction, quality, and clarity an hour's good rolling boil is usually adequate.

PITCHING THE YEAST

Fermentation takes place initially in a brewbin or plastic bag into which the wort is strained to leave behind any hops or grain.

The yeast cannot be "pitched" (added) until the temperature has dropped to 15.5°C (60°F) and if your time is likely to be short it is as well to make provision for the forced cooling of the wort by standing the boiler in a bath or sink of cold water or, if it is an electric one, to run a coil of hose through it from the cold water tap.

Do not pitch the yeast until the wort is tepid or the yeast may be killed.

Pitching the yeast

FERMENTATION

Fermentation will soon be vigorous as the yeast starts to consume the sugar in the wort, but it will be assisted if the wort is given a good rousing. Stir it vigorously with a large wooden spoon or paddle to get some oxygen into it before covering the bin with a cloth and then lightly replacing the lid. If using a bag, lightly tie the neck.

Keep the bin in a reasonably warm, but not hot, place (16–21°C, 60–70°F) and try to keep the temperature fairly constant, since this will assist a steady fermentation. Most houses nowadays have a spot where a brew can be kept at a satisfactory temperature—a few degrees are not critical—and that of a centrally heated house is almost certainly right.

A frothy mass of foam will soon build up on the surface, with some blobs of impurities which will adhere to the inside of the bin round the edge of the surface. Skim these off, together with the initial head which forms, to be gradually replaced (if you are using a good top-fermenting yeast) by a thick pancake of floating yeast. This does tend to cut off the oxygen supply to the wort, and it pays, with such a top-fermenting yeast, to admit some air to the brew, and also to agitate the "pancake" gently from below to keep live yeast circulating and without taking the dead yeast cells down into the brew. These yeasts ferment downwards as it were! If such a fermentation is kept closely covered the beer tends to acquire a rather sour taste.

If you are using a bottom fermenting yeast as when brewing lager the foregoing does not apply, and the brew can be kept more closely covered.

Strong beers will normally ferment out in a week to 10 days, weaker ones in three.

A good yeast pancake

RACKING AND RESTING

Many recipes and kits advocate bottling or casking the beer direct from the primary fermenter, and this can be done as long as the SG is below 1010 and preferably down to 1005. Bottling sooner may lead to burst bottles.

The snag with this direct bottling is that it usually results in too much yeast finishing up in the bottles. It is infinitely preferable to allow the beer to "rest" for six to seven days in a 5-gallon polypin, under an air lock, before priming and bottling.

When fermentation is finished rack (siphon) your beer into the polypin, being careful to leave all the yeast sediment behind; keep the tap of the lock uppermost and open, add any finings, and fit airlock as explained hereafter·

Note that it must not be used with the tap closed for fermenting, resting, or for storing beer once it has been primed, because it will not stand up to the pressures involved.

Siphoning from
fermenter to polypin

FINING

Finings can be added at this stage if desired. You can buy proprietary dry beer finings (which are usually gelatine) or buy gelatine in ½ oz. sachets ("Davis Gelatine"). Heat half a pint of water and stir the gelatine into it, but do not let it boil, then add it to the racked beer and stir or agitate the beer vigorously to mix the finings thoroughly with it. I find it helpful to have the finings ready before starting siphoning and to add a portion of them to successive gallons so that they are fairly evenly distributed.

Isinglass, sold as liquid beer finings, is much more sensitive to temperature and much more difficult to use, and I do not recommend it for that reason.

AIRLOCK

When you have fined the beer, jam a length of acrylic tubing into the open tap and lead it down into a milk bottle half filled with water, and you have an excellent air lock. Remember, the tap must be open!

In this way, any gas still being generated can be let out without bursting the polypin and the beer can be left to be dealt with at your leisure for days or even two or three weeks. A week's rest is usually enough, the great advantage being that more yeast can settle out, and the finings can render the beer star bright. The end result is that one has just a paint coat of yeast in the bottle instead of a thick layer.

Resting beer in a polypin

PRIMING

However you store your beer, in bottles or in keg, it must first be primed if it is to have that so desirable head and sparkle. This, of course, is brought about by a further brief fermentation in bottle or keg, and to achieve this the beer will need to be "primed" after its rest with a little, carefully-measured dose of sugar.

But first test your beer with a hydrometer to ensure that its SG is below 1010, and preferably 1005, or there may be too much sugar still present, in which case you will get a dangerous build-up of pressure in your bottles.

Priming sugar needs to be added at the rate of half a teaspoon (2.5 ml.) per pint or one *level* teaspoon (5 ml.) per quart. **Do not exceed this dose**, or you may have a Vesuvius when you open the bottle, or even a burst bottle.

For priming beer in bulk use equivalent amounts, 3 oz. to 5 gallons. (If you propose using an injector to serve the beer by pressure this can be reduced to 2 ozs.).

Priming . . .

BOTTLING

When you have collected your bottles, wash and sterilise them thoroughly and then funnel the exact amount of priming sugar into each one, half a teaspoon for pints, 1 level teaspoon for quarts. Work methodically, moving your funnel from bottle to bottle, so as to be sure that you do not double-dose any bottle by mistake.

Then siphon the beer into the bottles, letting it run gently down their sides to minimise foaming, and try to leave $\frac{3}{4}$ in. to 1 in. air space below the stopper or closure to provide expansion room to absorb some of the pressure which will be created.

Most beers, despite having been rested, will still carry traces of yeast in suspension, sufficient to attack the fresh sugar and effect an in-bottle fermentation but if you wish to make sure add a tiny quantity of fresh yeast, say two small "shot" per bottle.

Then seal your bottles with crown corks or screw stoppers using one of the splendid tools now available, and, if you wish, label them to increase their professional appearance.

It is useful, too, to devise some colour code for various types of brew—bitter, stout, lager etc. This is most easily done by using the various colours of crown caps that one can buy

Keep the bottles in a warm room for two days to encourage the fermentation, then move into a cool place, such as a larder, to assist clarification.

Bottling . . .   . . . and Capping

Do not drink your beer right away. It will need at least a fortnight in bottle to be drinkable and will improve for a month or so; clarity, bead (the tiny bubbles) head and flavour will all improve with true maturity and it may well be months before the beer really goes "over the hill" and its flavour starts to deteriorate.

Many brewers like using a modern device, the Beerbrite cap, which has a plastic blister to collect the yeast deposit which is inevitable in a naturally conditioned beer. The beer bottle is primed and inverted in a special stand, crate or rack, and by giving it an occasional jerk and twist the yeast is gradually shaken down into the blister—just as it is in the case of champagne. The cap is then bent in two and tied tightly with the twist-wire provided, sealing the yeast off from the beer.

Admittedly, the cap does not *look* very smart, but it is easy to overcome this by chilling the bottle in a refrigerator to reduce its gaseousness and then quickly replacing the blister cap with a crown closure. The resultant yeast-free, starbright beer is worth the extra trouble.

Similarly, if beer is well chilled, it can often be rebottled without too much loss of gas, enabling you to pour a beer clear to the last drop. Whether you are prepared to go to this trouble depends on how fussy you are, I suppose! With home brew so cheap most brewers feel they can afford to waste the last half inch or so clouded by sediment.

But generally this is unnecessary; if you feel so very aesthetic, it is far easier to use a pewter tankard. The beer will taste better and what the eye does not see . . . !

DRAUGHT BEERS

Partly because many brewers tire of endless bottle-washing and partly because of the difficulties of obtaining a sediment-free beer in bottle, the modern trend is, if anything, away from bottling in favour of the pressure barrel. There is nothing so satisfying as to be able to "draw off a pint" of your own!

PRESSURE BARRELS

With beer in a barrel, keg or pipkin, the lees are left at the bottom and clear beer is drawn off from above them. This way of dispensing beer has become much more popular nowadays because one can buy a variety of devices for pressurising barrels and kegs. The beer can be served under carbon dioxide pressure and no air need be admitted

The range of Weltonhurst barrels. The stand is to simplify dispensing

to the barrel, so that the beer will keep almost indefinitely. This is a big advantage; the only disadvantage is that beer takes much longer to clear in a cask or keg than it does in a bottle, since the yeast has further to fall, so fining with isinglass or gelatine is to be advocated.

To do this one needs a strong, pressure-resistant plastic barrel or keg—there are a dozen or so makes available—and it is also a good idea to invest in a CO_2 gas injection device to go with it to enable the beer to be dispensed to the last drop without contact with air.

Do not attempt to keep beer under pressure in polypins, and do not fiddle with old fashioned wooden beer barrels. They are difficult to maintain in good condition and the beer will almost certainly be flat before you can drink it all.

Of the custom-designed plastic barrels on the market several have now stood the test of time and you can safely invest in, say, one from Southampton Home Brews, a Hambleton Beer-sphere, a Rotokeg, a Saffron Superkeg or any of the Weltonhurst range of barrels as supplied to the trade. You can also use a "Drafty Five", a polypin specially designed for home brewers, incorporating a safety valve, but ordinary polypins will not stand up to the pressures involved.

Saffron Superkeg has many good features   The Rotokeg is fitted with a high level tap
and float system

INJECTORS

If you intend dispensing the beer by natural pressure you need to prime the bulk at the rate of 3 oz. of sugar to 5 gallons. The first few pints will draw splendidly, but eventually you will have to admit air from the top and you are likely to run into difficulty in keeping a head on the last few pints (unless you can dispose of 4 gallons at one sitting, which is by no means unknown in home brewing circles!).

Consequently, most brewers prefer to reduce the priming sugar to 2 oz., and back up the gas generated therefrom with a CO_2 injector using cartridges or cylinders. These are not called into operation until the "natural" pressure is exhausted, then the barrel can be given a quick squirt of gas from the injector, pressure is restored and, what is more, the beer is still protected from contact with air.

There are now many types of injector and tap on the market, all of them with individual advantages, and which one you use is largely a matter of personal preference. Generally speaking, the ones which use the larger cylinders of gas are preferable. They may be dearer to buy initially but are much cheaper to run, since one cylinder can do the work of 30 bulbs at 10p each, halving the cost of the actual gas.

Your local home brew shop can usually demonstrate the various types available and advise you in your choice.

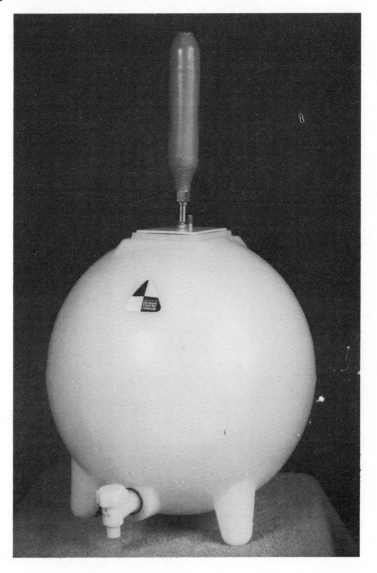

A Hambledon Bard Beersphere fitted with injector

CHAPTER 11

True Beers

Experienced home brewers are in little doubt that to obtain the highest-quality "true" beer one must do as the commercial brewery does, and employ grain malt and the mashing process. Mashing consists of soaking the "green" malt in hot water and converting its starch to fermentable sugar, maltose.

It is significant that in almost all the beer competitions which take place at national and regional level it is mashed grain beers that feature prominently in the prize lists, beers made almost entirely from malt grain and hops, with no added sugar.

(Anyone who is fortunate enough to have a holiday in Bavaria, and has an opportunity of sampling the beers there, where the use of sugar is forbidden by law, will appreciate what a true "malt and hops" aroma should be).

Any home brewer worth his salt will certainly want to try his hand at "true" beers, even if he does frequently, for convenience, turn to the employment of malt extract or brew from kits.

Some home brewers go so far as to try malting their own barley, but it is a tricky process and the chances of success are extremely small. It is far better to find a reliable supplier and purchase good-quality, ready-kilned malt, remembering that the bulk of the malt you will use should be *pale* malt, and that other malts are required mainly only for colouring and flavour changes. In mild and brown beers they will be used in quite small proportions and at the most, as when making a stout, will only be a quarter of the total malt used. The really dark malts contribute hardly any sugar at all.

When devising one's own recipes using grain malt it is essential to know how much maltose is likely to be obtained from any particular batch, since malts can vary enormously. This, if one is using a mixture of grains, can be somewhat complicated, since a series of tests and a proportion calculation will be required. The simplest plan is to work on the basis that the bulk of the malt used will be pale malt—as it will—and ignore the contribution to specific gravity made by the small amounts of other grain malts.

Good pale malt will yield four fifths of its own weight as sugar, others less.

One does certainly need to assess the potential of the pale malt, and it is simplest to do this so as to arrive at a result in terms of the gravity produced by the use of 1 lb. of malt per gallon. Having discovered this, it is a matter of simple multiplication to decide how much malt per gallon one needs to use to arrive at any desired original gravity.

MALT TEST

A simple test will obviate wasting hours of time in perhaps fruitless mashing. Take 2 oz. of your crushed pale malt and put it into a saucepan, add half a pint of water heated to 155°F., and hold the temperature as nearly as possible at 150°F. for an hour. Add a further half a pint of water at the same temperature and then allow to cool to just above 60°F. Strain through a coarse filter and check the specific gravity with your hydrometer. This will give the gravity resulting from the use of 1 lb. of that particular malt to the gallon. If your test, for instance, produces a gravity of 30, each ounce contributes roughly 2 degrees of gravity $(30 \div 16)$. From this it is easy to calculate how much malt will be required to be certain of reaching the gravity you desire. Any malt, incidentally, which produces a gravity of less than 23 in this test is not really worth using

PALE MALT

So it is important to purchase malt of the highest possible quality, clean and free of dust and rubbish, and with good, plump grains of uniform size, so that they will crush easily. The inside should be white and powdery if you crack it open and should taste distinctly of malt if bitten. Good pale malt has a light golden or straw colour. "Lager malt" is the continental equivalent, but not so good.

Pale malts and some malt extracts are diastatic, that is to say they can convert to sugar the starch in any other grain mashed with them. Some can convert as much as a third of their own weight. But the more heavily a malt is kilned, i.e. the darker it is, the more its diastatic ability is damaged, and heavily roasted or black malts have none at all, all their enzymes having been destroyed. They therefore contribute no sugar or conversion power to the mashing process.

If you locate a good pale malt, buy as much as you can afford, for it keeps well, but it is always as well to make a trial brew with a small quantity first.

DARKER MALTS

As already explained, (p. 46) one can buy various darker malts, and generally these are employed either to obtain darker beers or to effect subtle flavour changes.

OTHER GRITS AND ADJUNCTS

The starch in green malt is converted to sugar during mashing by the enzyme diastase. Diastase is sufficiently powerful to convert not only the starch of the malt, but that of any other grain (or "grit") that is added to it; a malt which has this ability to a great degree is described as "highly diastatic". We can take advantage of this and reduce the cost—or increase the strength—of our brews by including in the mash a proportion of other grains, or "grits" as they are called in commercial brewing—maize, oats, rice or wheat. They are best employed to make subtle flavour changes, and therefore used in small quantities.

Roast barley (unmalted) is excellent in dry stouts, as is *flaked Barley*. Other flaked grains—like breakfast cereals—are available; *Flaked Maize* and *Flaked Rice*, for instance, are good in light dry beers and lagers, the maize flavour being useful in Carlsberg-type lagers and rice in American-style beers such as Coors and Budweiser, as can be seen from the formulation on the can of the latter. *Malted Wheat* or *Torrified Wheat* can sometimes be found, but do not seem to have much practical advantage, and *Rolled Oats* are rarely used now that "oatmeal stout" like "milk stout", has gone out of fashion. A point worth noting is that if you cannot buy these adjuncts from home brew sources, some breakfast foods will do just as well— Shredded Wheat and Weetabix (wheat), cornflakes (maize) and Rice Krispies, for instance.

Another useful material is *Brumore*, a wheat flour widely used in commercial breweries. In the mashing context, malt extract can also be regarded as an adjunct and used to reduce cost.

As long as the proportion of adjuncts is kept low they can be mashed with the bulk of the pale malt, but if larger quantities are used they must be cooled separately first.

For instance, $\frac{1}{2}$ lb. of crushed maize or ground rice, and $\frac{1}{4}$ lb. malt can be heated in $\frac{1}{2}$ gallon of water to 45°C. (113°F.) and held at this temperature for half-an-hour, then boiled for a quarter-of-an-hour. This can then be mixed with a main mash, consisting say, of $1\frac{1}{2}$ lb. malt which has been steeped in half a gallon of water at 38°C. (100°F.) and kept at 30°C. (86°F.) for another hour. Mashing then proceeds in the usual way.

The comparative starch contents, as percentages of dry substances, in a few common "grits" are: Maize rice, 80–85; polished rice, 88–92; tapioca, 75–90; wheat, 65–78; potatoes, 65–75; oats, 60–70; rye 60–65; and barley, 57–65. Some of these are often used to add body and strength to a thin beer. It is as well, however, to avoid this particular commercial practice, since the economy is not great and the risks of making poor beers, which do not ferment or clear well, are much increased.

CRACKING

Before you can mash it, your malt must be cracked, to render the starch freely available, and it should be noted that "cracked" means what is says, i.e. crushed, rather than ground to a fine flour, which will make clarification difficult. If the husks can be left whole they later form a natural filter bed. So a device which will grind or crack only coarsely is required. I find a hand coffee mill of the hold fashioned type an ideal tool, the only trouble being that its hopper and receiving drawer are too small. A useful idea for a handyman is to remove the central grinding mechanism and build it into a larger hopper over a larger receptacle, such as a plastic bucket. The top part of a large polythene funnel makes an admirable hopper, or one can be constructed out of plywood.

A home-made malt crusher, plans for which are given in "Woodwork for Winemakers". It utilises an old fashioned wooden rolling pin

Alternatively, you may care to make the simple hand-operated crusher illustrated here for which Derek Smith and Colin Dart give full instructions and plans in their little book "Woodwork for Winemakers". This is constructed around an old-fashioned type wooden rolling pin.

An electric coffee mill is quite good, if adjustable, but otherwise tends to grind the malt too finely. One can also improvise by using a wooden rolling pin, or beer bottle as a roller, but this is apt to be rather a messy business, since grain tends to shoot everywhere, unless enclosed in a strong polythene or linen bag.

An ordinary hand mincer can also be useful

MASHING

The crushed malt has then to be mashed to convert its starch to maltose, or sugar, and to extract it. Ideally, one needs a long mashing period, as much as eight hours, to obtain the fullest conversion and extraction, but many home brewers content themselves with a two-hour mashing, since it is in the first two hours that the major enzymatic activity occurs.

Mashing is the central and most important single process in brewing, and both the consistency of the mash and temperature control are vital if optimum conversion of starch and extraction are to be achieved.

The temperature of the mash should be between 62°C. (145°F.) and 68°C. (155°F.) and should never be allowed to rise above the latter figure. The best rule of thumb is to aim at an average of 65°C. (150°F.), within one or two degrees, and to go as high as 65°C. (153°F.) for light ales and bitter, or as low as 63°C. (146°F.) for milds and browns. Temperature control is tricky, but can be achieved without too much difficulty, as will be seen.

If you are adopting the orthodox "mashing and sparging" method on no account use more than one gallon of liquor to 1½ lb. malt for the two purposes combined, or you will extract more starch than you can convert and finish up with a beer which has a starch haze.

You will have worked out how much malt you need to use to produce the desired quantity of beer, but your initial mash needs to be a stiff one, with at least 4½ lb. of malt to a gallon of liquor.

Normally, if brewing a four or five gallon batch, it is necessary to use two gallons or so of water to mash the grain, and the remainder also hot, for "sparging" or rinsing it, so as to finish up with the correct quantity, or "length".

There are three basic ways in which you can mash, and successfully maintain the desired temperature accurately throughout by using:
a) A large saucepan or "dixie" (up to 3 gallons) on a source of heat or in an oven.
b) A 2-gallon plastic bucket and an immersion heater.
c) A Bruheat boiler and a grain bag.

In a saucepan

Usually you will be using pale malt, some cereal adjuncts and perhaps some malt extract, and if you are using a saucepan they can all go in together.

You will need a really large saucepan—for years I used very successfully an old fashioned Army "dixie"—and you need to allow a pint of water for each pound of grain or diastatic malt extract. Heat the water to 55°C. (131°F.) and mix in the malt extract, followed by the grain malt and any adjuncts. Insert your thermometer and increase the heat to raise the temperature of the mash gradually to 68°C. (155°F.), stirring all the time to keep the mash from contact with the heated metal. Really thorough stirring is also always essential in any method of mashing, to prevent "dry spots," which are surprisingly persistent.

Switch off the heat and the mash will (very slowly) begin to cool, so keep an eye on your thermometer. Remember that your aim is to maintain an average temperature of 65°C. (150°F.) for the next hour or so, so you can allow yourself to work in the range 62°C. (145°F.) to 68°C. (155°F.). When the temperature drops to 62°C., therefore, apply more heat, and stir again, to bring the temperature back to 68°C. You will probably need to do this only two or three times.

One way of maintaining temperature easily is to put your large saucepan or dixie containing the hot mash in the gas oven (all shelves removed) on Regulo mark "low", or in electric oven set to maintain 62–68°C.

IODINE TEST

After half an hour or so test whether conversion is complete and you have reached "Starch End Point". Drop a small sample of mash on to a white tile or plate and add to it a few drops of iodine. It should remain brown; if there is any trace of blue or blue-black there is still some starch remaining and mashing must be continued, a second test can be made after a further quarter of an hour. When the sample remains brown conversion is complete.

Doing the iodine test

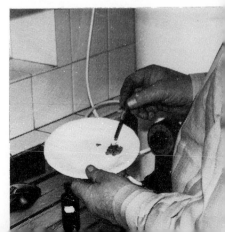

Making up the mash

Checking the temperature and mashing on an electric ring

Another way: mash in the oven

If all the starch has been successfully converted the mash must then be strained into your boiler and "sparged" (rinsed) with the remaining water, also at 68°C., until you have the volume of beer you intended making. This you can do by scooping up the mash in a nylon flour sieve and rinsing it through with two or three kettles full of hot water, as you would when cooking rice.

In a bucket

You can mash in a 2-gallon plastic bucket by employing a 50-watt immersion heater obtainable from home brew firms and it is best to have as liquid a mash as possible in this case to avoid the grain being in contact with the heater. This means, again, constant agitation and care that the heater does not touch the side or bottom of the bucket.

Some home brewers find close temperature control tedious, and adopt short cuts which, whilst perhaps not producing immaculate results, are still satisfactory. The method is to infuse the malt in some of the liquor, and maintain an even temperature by means of a thermostat, making possible much longer mashing periods.

Here is an example:

Use a 2-gallon polythene bucket or boiler, with lid. Bring just under two gallons of liquor to 65°C. (150°F.), pour them in the bucket, and scatter in 2 lb. of milled malt, or grist.

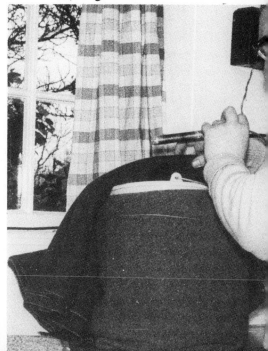

Yet another way: mashing in a bucket

Then insert a 50-watt glass immersion heater, put the lid on the bucket, cover with a blanket or thick cloth, and leave on overnight or for a period of eight hours. The temperature with these quantities and with this type of heater will remain between 54°C. (130°F.) and 65°C. (150°F.) and extraction is first rate. Such a heater, costing little, will last for years and it is quite unnecessary even to have a thermostat; current consumption is negligible.

Strain off into a boiler and sparge to three, or even four, gallons. Add 2 oz. hops and 2 lb. block invert sugar. Boil for an hour. Strain, cool to 75°F., ferment, prime and bottle as usual.

In the Bruheat

You may, however, be lucky enough to have a boiler with a tap, and in this case the job can be greatly simplified, particularly if it is a Bruheat, as sold by Ritchie Products, which is custom built for the job. It is a large polypropylene bucket fitted with a tap, electric element and thermostat, and is absolutely ideal for mashing, since it will hold the mash at a constant temperature. The Bruheat is light and easy to handle, and the electrical system dismantles easily and safely, so a thorough cleaning can be done after every use. It is therefore the best possible brewing tool.

Use about two gallons of your total of four or five for mashing. Pour it into the boiler and switch on, and as it warms pour in any malt extract that you are using. Your pale grain malt and other grist such as cereal flakes are best contained in a grain bag of reasonably fine mesh, suspended in the boiler so that the grain is below the surface of the liquid but clear of the element. Keep the top of the bag open so that you can stir the mash with a large spoon or ladle.

Turn up the heat and keep stirring until you reach the magic mashing level of 65°C., then turn the dial of the thermostat slowly back until you can discover where it clicks on and off at that temperature, leave it there, and the Bruheat is then set, and will maintain the mash at that temperature indefinitely.

When conversion is shown to be complete by the iodine test lift the grain bag clear of the wort and sparge with the remaining liquor, also at 65°C.

Using a Bruheat a suitable recipe for five gallons bitter is: 7 lb. crushed pale malt, $\frac{1}{2}$ lb. crushed crystal malt, 3 oz. Goldings hops, 2 lb. brewing sugar (Itona), 1 teaspoon Leigh Williams pale ale water treatment (if you live in a soft water district). Dry beer finings.

SPARGING

Whichever way you decide to mash, at the end of the process you will need to strain your wort into a boiler. Stretch a grain bag or nylon netting over the top of the boiler and secure it around the rim, and tip the mash into it. If, on the other hand, you have used a grain bag in the boiler lift it clear of the wort and suspend it similarly.

Then "sparge", or rinse, the mash gently with the remainder of the liquor, which should be at a temperature of 75°C. (170°F.) or so at the outset to maintain that 65°C. (150°F.) mashing temperature, and the wort running out should be at that temperature. If it is not, increase the temperature of the sparging liquor or turn up the heat. For sparging use a very fine watercan hose or a (clean!) garden pressure spray so that you can do it gently. This is rather a slow job, and to my mind the only tedious part of the mashed-beer process. I preheat the sparging liquor and then use it, a gallon at a time, from a watering can.

BRUHEAT BITTER

As an example of the mashing and sparging technique try "Bruheat Bitter."

Using a Bruheat a suitable recipe for five gallons bitter is: 7 lb. crushed pale malt, ½ lb. crushed crystal malt, 3 oz. Goldings hops, 2 lb. brewing sugar (Itona), 1 teaspoon Leigh Williams pale ale water treatment (if you live in a soft water district). Dry beer finings.

BREWING
BRUHEAT
BITTER

(See previous page)

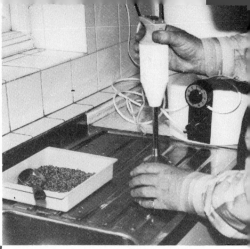

1. Cracking the malt with an electric mill

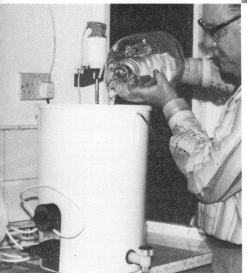

2. Mashing in Bruheat. Pouring water

3. The malt is placed in a strong grain bag ▶

94

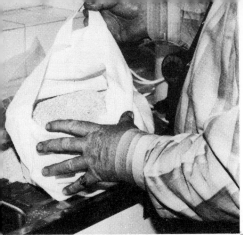

4. . . . which is then closed and suspended in the liquor

5. The mash must be frequently and thoroughly stirred to avoid dry spots ▶

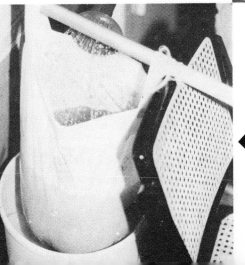

6. Sparging: Bag supported on a rod between sink unit and chair back; hot water sprayed on mash from watering can

7. An alternative way of sparging, using sieve and jug ▶

◀ **8. Adding brewing sugar to the wort**

9. Putting hops in bag ▶

10. Adding hops to brew ▶

BOILING

Once sparging is complete the wort must be thoroughly boiled to extract the flavour from the hops which are now added to it, to obtain the essential bitterness of beer. Any sugars used in the recipe can also be added at this stage. Use $\frac{1}{2}$ oz. to $1\frac{1}{2}$ oz. of hops per gallon, according to the degree of bitterness required, but hold back a small quantity to add in the last five minutes. (The aroma of the hops tends to be boiled out; this will restore it.) It is a good idea to enclose the hops loosely in a nylon net bag with a long string, for easy removal later. The wort must be boiled for at least half an hour, and preferably three-quarters, and one point to note is that boiling does darken the beer (half an hour will give a pale beer, but less will give an anaemic-looking one, and up to $1\frac{1}{2}$ hours will produce a darker beer). For stouts and extra stouts, of course, black malt should be used. **A good rolling boil is essential.**

FERMENTING

When the temperature has dropped to 15.5°C. (60°F.) strain off or remove the hops, give the wort a good rousing, and run it off into your fermenting bin. It pays to fit a scrap of nylon pot scourer in the inside end of the tap to prevent odd bits of grain or hops causing a blockage. Or protect the inlet with your long-handled spoon or a flour sieve. Pitch the yeast, and ferment, rest, prime and bottle as usual.

THE MASHED BEER PROCESS SUMMARISED

1. Grind your malt and grits.
2. Bring two gallons or so of water to 68°C. (155°F.) and dissolve in it any diastatic malt extract.
3. Mash it in your malt and grits, in a grain bag if necessary, at an average temperature of 65°C. (150°F.).
4. Test with iodine to ensure conversion is complete.
5. Strain into boiler; sparge with remaining water, at 65°C.
6. Add hops, any sugars, or plain malt extract.
7. Boil for at least an hour, adding a few hops in the last five minutes.
8. Cool, add yeast, ferment as usual.
9. Rack, rest and bottle.

LAGER
(4 gallons)

Ingredients:

4 lb.	Pale malt (cracked)	2 kilo
2½ oz.	Hallertauer hops	70 g.
3 lb.	Sugar	1.3 kg.
	Lager yeast	
½ teaspoon	Citric acid	
4 gallons	Water (soft)	18 litres

Method:

Mash as described, using two gallons of water, in a Bruheat, with the malt in a suspended brewbag. Then strain the wort into the boiler, add 2 oz. hops, the salt, and the remaining water, bring to the boil, and simmer for 40 minutes. Add a few loose hops (½ oz. or so). Simmer for five minutes.

Put the sugar and the citric acid into a 5-gallon polythene brewbin and strain on to them the wort. Add the balance of the water, cold, and stir thoroughly until all sugar is dissolved. Cool to 75°F., then add lager yeast and nutrient.

Lager yeast is a bottom fermenter, i.e. it will eventually settle well. The first head of froth which forms on the brew after two days should be skimmed off. Fermentation will normally take a week in a warm place. Keep the container well covered. Bottle when S.G. is about 1005 and certainly not above 1010, or when surface of brew clears but tiny bubbles are visible in a ring in the middle. Add one level teaspoon sugar to each quart flagon, fill to within ¼ in. of stopper, and screw down well. Store upright in cool place for at least a month.

And here is a recipe by Dave Line which makes 2 gallons of Pilsner type lager (OG32) and 2 gallons of strong lager simultaneously. Brew 4 gallons of the low gravity lager, keep 2 as Pilsner, and add Golden Syrup to ferment the remainder to a strong brew.

PILSNER TYPE LAGER

Ingredients:

4 lb.	Crushed lager malt	2 kilo
1 lb.	Flaked maize	450 g.
2 lb.	Golden syrup	1 kilo
2½ oz.	Hallertauer hops	70 g.
	Lager yeast	
	Soft water (remove chalk by pre-boiling if necessary)	

Method:

Heat 3 gallons of water up to 51–54°C. (125–130°F.) and stir in the crushed lager malt and flaked maize. Leave to stand for half an hour.

Stirring continuously, slowly raise the temperature of the mash up to 65°C. (150°F.) and leave it again, ensuring that the mash stays as near to, but not exceeding, 65°C. for another half an hour or so until Starch End Point is passed.

Strain off from the grain (best held in a large grain bag) and sparge (rinse) with hot water around 71°C. (160°F.) to collect 4 gallons of liquid.

Boil the wort with 1½ ozs. of the hops for 1½ hours. Switch off and stir in the rest of the hops. Stir the hops in the wort two or three more times over the next quarter of an hour.

Strain off into a fermenting bin, taking care to leave the hops and protein debris behind. Top up with cold water to the 4 gallon mark.

When cool to 15°C. (60°F.), pitch a working lager yeast starter. Try to maintain the temperature below 17°C. (65°F.) to avoid off flavours from the bottom fermenting yeast. Skim off any dirty yeast that forms.

After 4–5 days when the S.G. falls to around 7, rack off into a polythene cube and add gelatine finings.

Two days later prepare four one gallon jars. To each of two of them add 1 lb. of golden syrup dissolved in the same volume of warm water.

Siphon the clear beer in to the gallon jars and fit airlocks.

The two jars without the syrup contain the Pilsner lager which can be bottled after another week's rest. Besides priming each bottle with sugar, "Krausen" with a few grains of lager yeast. Mature for one month in the bottle before drinking.

The special brew lager will ferment for another week using up the golden syrup. When fermentation abates, rack off into other gallon jars and let it rest for two weeks before bottling.

This time 'dunk' the siphon tube momentarily into the yeast sediment to carry over sufficient cells to act on the priming sugar. This one is worth maturing for at least two months in the bottle before drinking.

100

LONDON LIGHT ALE
(5 gallons, 22 litres)

Ingredients:

4 lb.	Crushed pale malt	1.8 kg.
½ lb.	Flaked rice	230 gm.
1 lb.	Glucose chips	450 gm.
2 oz.	Goldings hops	60 gm.
	Beer yeast	

Method:

Collect 2 gallons (9 litres) of water from hot tap and add ½ tsp. of lactic acid water treatment. Mix in the ground pale malt and flaked rice. Mash as directed, sparge to collect 3 gallons of wort. Boil the wort with the hops for 1 hour before straining off into the fermentation bin. Stir in the glucose chips until dissolved. Top up to 5 gallons with cold water. When cool, add the yeast and ferment until the S.G. falls to 1.007 before racking off into a polythene cube.

CLASSIC PALE ALE
Five gallons at O.G. of 45

5 lb.	Crushed pale malt	2.25 kilo
2 lb.	D.M.S. malt extract	1 kg.
4 oz.	Brewing flour	100 g.
2 oz.	Fuggles hops	50 g.
3 oz.	Goldings hops	90 g.
1 lb.	Glucose chips	450 g.
	Water treatment for Pale Ale	
	Irish Moss	
	Commercial brewing yeast (if possible)	
	from Worthington White Shield or	
	draught Whitbread Trophy.	

Method:

Add the water treatment to three gallons (13.5 litres) of water and raise the temperature to 65°C. (150°F.). Dissolve the malt extract in the hot water. Dry mix the brewing flour and the cracked pale malt and then slowly stir this in as well. Continue stirring whilst raising the temperature of these goods slowly (say over five minutes) back to 65°C. Mash for two hours. Sparge (rinse) the grains with hot water to collect 4½ gallons (20 litres) of wort.

Measure out 1 oz. (30 g.) of the Goldings hops and add these with the Fuggles to the wort and boil for at least one hour. Use the Irish Moss as directed in the instructions. Switch off the boiler and allow the solids to settle. Hold the remaining 2 oz. (55 g.) of Goldings in a large grain bag or strainer below the boiler tap. Position a collection vessel below the strainer. Crack open the boiler tap and let the hot wort percolate gently through the hops to extract some of their finer flavouring properties.

Dissolve the glucose chips in a few pints of hot water and add this to the fermenting bin as well. Top up the wort to five gallons (22 litres) with preboiled water. When the wort cools to 20°C. (70°F.) stir in a yeast starter cultivated from a commercial yeast.

Ferment four to five days until the S.G. falls to 12 and then rack off into a five gallon "ex-wine" polythene cube fitted with an airlock. Add ½ oz. of Gelatine in solution for fining. Bottle four days later in primed beer bottles.

ECONOMY PALE ALE
(2½ gallons)

Ingredients:

½ lb.	**Crushed maize or ground rice**	**225 g.**
1¾ lb.	**Malt**	**900 g.**
2½	**Gallons water**	**11 litres**
	Yeast	
1½ oz.	**Golding hops**	**50 g.**

Method:

Make your main mash by steeping 1½ lb. cracked malt in half a gallon of water at 38°C. (101°F.) for quarter of an hour and keep at 30°C. (86°F.) for a further hour. Meanwhile crack ½–1 lb. of maize (or rice) and ¼ lb. malt with a rolling pin or mincer, put into half a gallon of water and bring up to 45°C. (113°C.). Hold at this temperature for half an hour, then boil for a further quarter of an hour. Mix your two mashes. Raise the temperature to 72°C. (160°F.) for the starch to sugar conversion to proceed, and when this is complete, as shown by an iodine test heat the brew to 75°C. (167°F.) to stabilise it. The solids should then be allowed to settle and the clear wort is then run off and made up to 2½ gallons with more water. Add 2 oz. hops, a teaspoon of salt, bring to the boil, and simmer for two hours. Cool to 20°C. (70°F.), pitch the yeast, ferment and bottle as usual.

STRONG PALE ALE
(4 gallons)

Ingredients:

4 lb.	**Malt**	**2 kilo**
6 lb.	**Sugar**	**3 kilo**
4 oz.	**Golding hops**	**100 g.**
4 gallons	**Water (hard)**	**18 litres**
	Brewer's yeast	

Method:

Crack the malt.

Measure out four gallons of water and bring two gallons (9 litres) of it to 65°C. (150°F.). Put the malt into 2-gallon polythene bucket and pour on to it as much water as possible. Insert 50-watt immersion heater, cover and wrap bucket with blanket, and switch on. Leave heater on for eight hours, keeping the temperature of the liquor at about 65°C. (150°F.). Then strain the wort into a boiler, add 3 oz. hops, and the salt, bring to the boil, and simmer for 40 minutes. Add another 1 oz. hops and simmer for further, five minutes.

Put the sugar into a polythene brewbin and strain on to it the wort through a nylon sieve. Stir well, bring the quantity up to four gallons with cold water, and stir thoroughly to make sure all sugar is dissolved. Allow to cool to 70°F., then cream your yeast in a pudding basin half filled with the wort, and pour this barm back into the brew. Ferment and continue as usual, priming and bottling after 9 or 10 days.

BIRMINGHAM ALE
(4 gallons)

Ingredients:

4 lb.	**Pale malt (crushed)**	**2 kilo**
3 oz.	**Goldings hops**	**85 g.**
4 gallons	**Water (Birmingham's is said to be excellent for this brew).**	**18 litres**
2 lb.	**Crystal malt (cracked)**	**1 kilo**
1½ lb.	**Brewing sugar**	**700 g.**
	Yeast: cultured from 2 bottles of Guinness	

Method:

Bring about six pints water to 170°F. and pour into warmed enamel bucket, add the grain and test temperature, if this has dropped below 65°C. (150°F.) raise to this figure with hot water until temperature is uniform throughout the mash. Place in gas oven (all shelves removed) on Regulo mark "low", leave to mash for two hours.

Now strain into boiler, add water to four gallons and the brewing sugar and the hops, but keep back about ½ oz. of the latter until later. Boil for two hours then add the ½ oz. of hops and simmer for five minutes.

Strain into fermenting bin and leave to cool to 70°F.

Take S.G. This should be about 40–45° which will give a potential alcoholic content of 4½%. Pitch yeast and ferment down to 10° before barrelling (about three days). Prime with 16 level teaspoonsful of castor sugar and add about one-third of a pint of Leigh-Williams Beer Finings.

"AMBER GLOW" STOCK ALE
3 gallons (15 litres) Original Gravity 1066

Ingredients:

4 lb.	Crushed pale malt	2 kilo
1 lb.	Crushed amber malt	500 gm.
2 lb.	Demerara sugar	1 kilo
4 oz.	Fuggles hops	125 gm.
3 teaspoon	Formula 67 yeast	15 ml.
½ tsp./pint	White sugar	5 ml./litre

Method:

Use permanently hard water, mashing in 2½ gallons and collecting after sparging, three gallons of liquid. Boil with the hops for 1½ hours and strain off into a fermenting vessel. Add sugar dissolved as a syrup. When cool, pitch in the yeast and ferment and bottle as usual.

TRADITIONAL BITTER
4 gallons (20 litres) Original Gravity 1045

Ingredients:

7 lb.	Crushed pale malt	3500 gm.
4 oz.	Hallertau hops	125 gm.
	Leigh Williams hop powder	
2 oz.	Brown sugar	60 gm.
	Beer yeast	
	Beer finings	

Method:

Mix the crushed malt with hot tap water to form a smooth porridge. Raise the temperature to 68°C. (155°F.) and mash for another hour. Strain off the hot wort and rinse the grains gently to collect four gallons of liquid. Add the hops and boil for $1\frac{1}{2}$ hours. Carefully strain off the clear wort from the hops and protein debris. Top up to the final quantity with cold water.

Ferment and finish as usual.

CRYSTAL CROWN BITTER
(Five gallons)

Crystal Crown is an excellent best draught bitter brewed with the minimum of fuss and time. Although it is a grain beer using mashing techniques, it can be brewed in an evening quite easily.

7 lb.	Crushed pale malt	3 kg.
5 oz.	Crushed crystal malt	150 g.
4 oz.	Brewing flour	100 g.
2 oz.	Bramling Cross (OT48) or Fuggles hops	55 g.
3 oz.	Best Goldings hops	85 g.
2 lb.	Golden Syrup	1 kilo
2 tablespoon	Sticky molasses	
	Yeast starter from Guinness bottle dregs	
	Irish Moss	
	Lactic acid water treatment	

Some brewing flour is included to increase the head retention of the beer. Where chalky waters are encountered, a teaspoonful of lactic acid can speed up the reactions. This is added to three gallons of water in the Bruheat after the temperature has reached 150°F. Slowly stir in the grains premixed with the flour, ensuring that there are no dry spots. Increase the heat setting and stir the goods continuously until the temperature reaches 150°F. again. Taking this extra care at the start of mashing should ensure that the Starch End Point is passed within half an hour so long as the temperature is maintained at 144–150°F.

Transfer the goods after one hour's mashing to the grain bag and sparge with hot water to collect $4\frac{1}{2}$ gallons of wort. Return the wort to the boiler and boil vigorously for 45 minutes *without the hops*. Use the Irish Moss in the boil as directed on the instructions. Switch off the boiler and stir in hops. Give the hops two or three more stirs at five minute intervals before allowing them to settle.

Please restrain your natural brewing instinct and don't be tempted to boil the hops.

Strain off the wort and add the golden syrup and molasses dissolved first in a few pints of hot water. Molasses can be purchased in Health Food shops in 1½ lb. tins containing the thick, dark, coarse textured sugar syrup. Top up to five gallons with cold water.

When cool add the yeast, and ferment, rack, rest prime and barrel as usual.

WHITBREAD TROPHY STYLE BITTER
(5 gal. Original gravity 1037 25 litre.)

4 lb.	Crushed pale malt	2 kilo
5 oz.	Torrefied barley	150 gm.
2½ gallons	Water for "bitter" brewing	12 lit.
1 teaspoon	Irish moss	5 ml.
1 lb.	Barley syrup	500 gm.
1 lb.	Soft dark brown sugar	500 gm.
2 oz.	Fuggles hops	60 gm.
$(1+\frac{1}{4}+\frac{1}{4})$oz.	Goldings hops	(30+10+10) gm.
2 oz.	Brewers yeast	60 gm.
½ oz.	Gelatine	15 gm.
2 oz.	Brown sugar	60 gm.

Method:

Mash as usual and rinse the grains to collect 20 litres (4 gallons) of extract.

Boil the extract with the Fuggles hops and the first quota of Goldings hops for 1½ hours. Dissolve the main batch of sugar and barley syrup in a little hot water and add this during the boil. Also pitch in the Irish Moss as directed on the instructions.

Switch off the heat, stir in the second batch of Goldings and allow them to soak for 15 minutes. Strain off the clear wort into a fermenting bin and top up the final quantity with cold water.

Ferment, rack, rest and put into primed pressure barrel as usual.

BRIDGEND BITTER
(5 gallons. Starting gravity 1050)

Ingredients:

7 lb.	Crushed pale malt	3.2 kl.
12 oz.	Crushed crystal malt	340 gm.
4 oz.	Flaked barley	113 gm.
1 oz.	Crushed black malt	30 gm.
1 lb.	Golden syrup	450 gm.
1 teaspoon	Irish moss	5 gm.
2 oz.	Invert sugar (as priming sugar)	60 gm.
	Guinness yeast starter	
3 oz.	East Kent Golding hops	90 gm.
1 oz.	Progress hops	30 gm.
	Small handful Challenger hops or tea-spoon Hopfix 50 Golding (as dry hops)	
1 packet	Davis' Gelatine	

Method:

Mash the grain with 3 gallons of water for two hours to ensure a higher proportion of dextrinous sugars.

Sparge to collect 5 gallons (22 litres).

Boil with the hops and the golden syrup for two hours adding Irish Moss half way through the boil. (Northdown or good quality Fuggles will do if Progress is difficult to obtain but use less of Northdown).

Strain off the wort and cool rapidly to achieve the cold break. Top up with cold water to 5 gallons.

Pitch the yeast and stir vigorously to aerate the wort.

Thereafter continue as usual, fining with gelatine before putting beer into primed barrel.

BITTER
(4 gallons)

Ingredients:

2 lb.	Crystal malt	1 kilo
2 lb.	Tin Golden Syrup	1 kilo
	Beer Yeast	
2 lb.	Pale malt	1 kilo
3 oz.	Golding hops	85 g.
4 gallons	Water (hard)	18 litres

Method:
Mash the malts in the boiler at 65°C. (150°F.) for four hours. Strain off. Add the hops and salt and boil for an hour. Strain again and add the syrup. Allow to cool to 60–65°C. and add the yeast. Ferment at 17°C. and 20°C. for four days. Then prime and barrel as usual.

MILD ALE

Ingredients:

4 lb.	**Crystal malt (cracked)**	**2 kilo**
1 lb.	**Flaked maize**	**450 g.**
4 lb.	**Dark brown sugar**	**2 kilo**
4 gallons	**Water (soft)**	**18 litres**
1 dsrtspoon	**Caramel**	
4 oz.	**Hops**	**100 g.**
	Yeast and nutrient	
1 teaspoon	**Each salt and citric acid**	

Method:
The ale is best made by those living in a soft water district.
Crack the malt.
Measure out four gallons (18 litres) of water and bring 2 gallons (9 litres) to 65°C. (150°F.). Put the malt and flaked maize into 2-gallon polythene bucket and pour on to it as much water as possible. Insert 50-watt immersion heater and mash for eight hours at 65°C. (150°F.). Then strain the wort into a boiler, add $3\frac{1}{2}$ oz. hops, and the salt, bring to the boil, and simmer for 40 minutes. Add another $\frac{1}{2}$ oz. hops and the caramel (Crosse & Blackwell's liquid gravy browning) and simmer for further five minutes.

Put the sugar into a polythene dustbin, with the citric acid, and strain on to it the wort through a nylon sieve. Bring the quantity up to four gallons with cold water, and stir thoroughly to make sure all sugar is dissolved. Allow to cool to 70°F., then cream your yeast in a pudding basin half filled with the wort, and pour this barm back into the brew. Cover closely and leave in a warm place for eight to ten days. Ferment out, rest, prime and bottle as usual.

BROWN ALE (1)

Ingredients:

8 oz.	Crystal malt (cracked)	225 g.
1 lb.	black malt (lightly cracked)	450 g.
3 oz.	Fuggles hops	85 g.
4 gallons	Water (soft)	18 litres
1 lb.	Brewing flour	450 g.
4 lb.	DMS malt extract	2 kilo
1 lb.	Invert sugar	450 g.
4	Vinotex yeast tablets	

Method:

Follow normal mashing procedure. If you wish to increase the body add, say, 8 oz. (450 g.) flaked barley.

BROWN ALE (2)

Ingredients:

5 lb.	Pale malt	2.25 kilo
4 lb.	Roasted malt	2 kilo
2 lb.	Brewing sugar	1 kilo
2 teaspoons	Salt	
2½ oz.	Fuggles hops	70 g.
4 gallons	Water (softened if necessary)	18 litres
	Brewer's yeast	

Method:

Measure out your four gallons of water and bring up to 65°C. (150°F.) in a Bruheat boiler. Put the malt into a brewbag and infuse in the water. Leave heater on for two hours, keeping temperature between 62°C. (145 F.) and 68°C. (155°F.). Then lift out and drain the bag, add the hops and salt, bring to the boil and simmer for 40 minutes; add ½ oz. loose hops and simmer for further five minutes. Put the brewing sugar into a 5-gallon polythene brewbin, and strain the wort on to it through a nylon sieve. Stir well to amalgamate, then stir thoroughly again. Cool to 20°C. (70°F.) before adding the yeast and nutrient. Ferment and continue as usual.

BEST BROWN ALE
(5 gallons 25 litres)

5 lb.	**Crushed pale ale or mild ale malt**	2500 gm.
½ lb.	**Crushed wheat malt**	250 gm.
3½ oz.	**Crushed black malt**	110 gm.
½ lb.	**Demerara sugar**	250 gm.
1 lb.	**Glucose chips**	500 gm.
2½ oz.	**Hallertau hops**	75 gm.
1	**Sachet of dried beer yeast**	1
	Sweetex liquid	
	Heading liquid	

Method:

Mash the crushed malt in soft water between 145–155°F. for 1½ hours. Strain and sparge to collect 4 gallons of liquor. Boil with the hops for one hour and strain into a fermenting bin. Top up with the sugar quota in solution and cold water to the final quantity. When cool add the yeast and ferment 4–6 days until the S.G. falls to 1008. Rack off and keep under airlock protection for a few days before bottling. Add to each bottle ½ teaspoon of white sugar, one drop of heading liquid, one drop of Sweetex liquid per pint of capacity. Mature for two weeks before sampling.

BARLEY WINE
(1 gallon)
by P. Bryant

True "barley wine" can only be made successfully by using good quality pale malted barley as the main ingredient. Malt extract will never give the full, malty flavour required, whatever quantity is used.

The best adjunct to use is flaked rice or polished barley, which help to provide body. You can try flaked maize, cornflakes, ground rice oat flakes and dried bananas, but for this recipe one of the two abovementioned adjuncts is to be preferred.

Ingredients:

1¾ lb.	Pale malted barley	800 g.
2 oz.	Flaked rice or 4 oz. polished barley	55 g.
1 oz.	Hops	30 g.
1 lb.	Sugar	450 g.
1	Level teaspoon citric acid	
1 gallon	Water	4.5 litres
1	Level teaspoon ammonium sulphate	
1	Level teaspoon gypsum	
½ teaspoon	Salt	
1	Campden tablet	
	Champagne yeast	

Method:

Pick over and then put malted barley and adjunct through mincer to form the grist.

Heat one gallon of water to 68°C. in 12-pint saucepan on very low gas; add grist and mash for two hours.

Strain through kitchen sieve and then replace wort in saucepan, add hops and gypsum and boil for 40 minutes. Strain again, cool and take S.G., which should be around 48.

Add sugar, Campden tablet, citric acid, ammonium sulphate, salt and champagne yeast, and commence fermenting in a 2-gallon polythene bucket with lid. Fermentation will be strong within 12 hours. Skim brown scum from surface each day and after two days siphon into gallon jar and fit fermentation lock. When clearing begins (which may be after six weeks) rack and refit lock. When clear, rack again, cork, and store for six months, after which it may be bottled.

BARLEY WINE
(3 gallons)
by Wilf Newsom

Ingredients:

5 lb.	Pale malt	2.3 kilo
1 oz.	Black malt	30 g.
3 teaspoons	Gypsum	
	Demerara sugar to Gravity 83	
	Beer and Champagne yeast blended, and latterly a general purpose wine yeast	
1 lb.	Crystal malt	453 g.
4 oz.	Wheat syrup	120 g.
3½ oz.	Whitbread Golding hops	100 g.

Method:

Bring water to 65°C. (154°F.), add grist (crushed grains) and mash for 2 hours at 62–68°C. (144–154°F.),or to starch end point (clear wort). Strain off, add gypsum and hops and boil for 40 minutes. Strain off. Gravity should be approximately 48. Add sugar as syrup to a gravity of 83. When cool, add blend of active beer and champagne yeast. After skimming, transfer into 5 lit. (1 gal.) jars, fit airlocks and allow fermentation to proceed. When the gravity has reached the 20 mark the fermentation will show signs of stopping. At this stage pitch in activated General Purpose Wine Yeast and ferment out. Bottle and prime in nips of 180 ml. (6½ fl. oz.) 284 ml. (½ pt.). Keep for at least *12 months* before serving.

JUBILEE ALE
by Dave Line

2 gallons	O.G. 95
6 lb.	Crushed pale malt
2 lb.	Crushed lager malt
1 lb.	Soft brown sugar
3 oz.	East Kent Goldings
1 oz.	*Styrian Goldings or Bramling Cross hops
	C.W.E. Formula 67 yeast

A good permanently hard water is essential for mashing this grist. Add one teaspoonful of Gypsum to three gallons of mashing liquor.

Method:

Mash by the standard method and sparge to collect just over three gallons of wort.

Add the hops and sugar and boil the mix for at least an hour or until the volume has been reduced to 2½ gallons. Let the wort settle for 15 minutes after the boil before carefully straining off the clear wort from the bed of hops into an ex-wine polythene cube fitted with an airlock in the filler cap.

When cool the wort should have a gravity of between 90 and 100 to give the brew the alcohol potential of a table wine. Pitch in the wine yeast and ferment for a week or so until the vigorous activity abates. Complete the fermentation in two one-gallon jars. Just like normal wine procedures, rack the brew off the heavy sediment into fresh jars. Here the ale will eventually fall bright, leaving a thin deposit of yeast on the bottom.

Add two teaspoonfuls of white sugar dissolved in a little warm water to each of two fresh gallon jars. Rack the clear beer into them, ensuring a little yeast is carried over. Fit airlocks and wait for the fermentation to restart before bottling in nip or half pint bottles.

ANDOVER STOUT
(4 gallons/18 litres)

Ingredients:

4 lb.	**Pale malt (crushed)**	**2 kilo**
2 lb.	**Patent black malt**	**1 kilo**
2 lb.	**Crystal malt (crushed)**	**1 kilo**
2 lb.	**Brewing sugar, or Golden Syrup**	**1 kilo**
2½ oz.	**Fuggles hops**	**75 g.**
2 teaspoons	**Salt**	
½ teaspoon	**Citric acid**	
	Brewers yeast	
4 gallons	**Water (softened)**	

Method:

Mash the three malts in a brew-bag in two gallons (9 litres) of water in a Bruheat boiler.

Start with the water at 65°C. (150°F.) and set the boiler to hold the temperature at 62°C.–68°C. (145°F.–155°F.) for two hours. Then remove the bag and let it drain, make up to 4 gallons (18 litres), add 2 oz. hops, and salt, and bring to the boil. Boil for 40 minutes, add the remaining hops and boil for a further five. Put the Golden Syrup and citric acid into your brewbin and strain the wort on to them. Stir thoroughly. When cool, add the yeast starter, and continue as usual.

BIRMINGHAM STOUT

Ingredients:

4 lb.	Pale malt (crushed)	2 kilo
1 lb.	Roasted (or black) malt	450 g.
1½ lb.	brewing sugar	675 g.
3 oz.	Hops	85 g.
	Yeast (culture from two bottles of Guinness, see page 56)	
1 lb.	Crystal malt	450 g.
1 lb.	Flaked Barley	450 g.
1	level teaspoon salt	
4 gallons	Water	18 litres

Method:

As for Birmingham Ale (page 103).

MILK STOUT

Ingredients:

2 lb.	Patent black malt	1 kilo
6 oz.	Flaked barley	150 g.
2 lb.	Glucose (powdered)	1 kilo
4 gallons	Water (soft)	18 litres
4 lb.	Pale malt (crushed)	2 kilo
	Brewing yeast	
2 oz.	Hops	55 g.
1 teaspoon	Salt	

Method:

Culture a stout or Guinness yeast (see page 56). Failing this, buy a good quality beer yeast.

Bring two gallons of water up to 150°F., in a boiler and mash the malts and barley as described. (the black malt gives your stout the desired dark colouring and woody tang, while the barley, or grit, provides extra strength economically). Then strain the wort back into the boiler, add 1½ oz. of hops and the salt, bring to the boil and simmer for 40 minutes. Add the remaining ½ oz. of hops and simmer for five minutes. Put the 2 lb. powdered glucose into a brewbin and strain the wort on to them. Stir thoroughly, bring the total volume up to four gallons by adding the remainder of the water, cold, and stir again.

When cool, add the yeast starter and stand container, closely covered, in a warm place. The fermentation will be going well after 48 hours; skim on the third day. Ferment, rest, prime and bottle as usual.

SWEET STOUT
(5 gallons)

Ingredients:

3½ lb.	**Pale malt**	**1.6 kilo**
6 oz.	**Crystal malt**	**180 g.**
3½ oz.	**Whitbread Golding hops**	**105 g.**
	Beer yeast	
½ lb.	**Lamberts silcose caramel**	**230 g.**
8 oz.	**Porage oats**	**240 g.**
	Sweetex (liquid)	
	Demerara sugar to 1.035°	

Method:

Crush malts, add oats, and mash at 58°C. (138°F.). When starch-free, run off wort and boil with hops and Silcose for 35 minutes. Add sugar as syrup until S.G. 1.035 is reached. Chill rapidly add active yeast and ferment out at 15°C. (60°F.). Just before bottling, taste beer. Add Sweetex to taste (four drops equal 1 teaspoon of sugar). As this is an unfermentable sweetening agent there is no danger of further fermentation. Bottle and prime in the normal way. Keep for four weeks before serving.

IRISH TYPE STOUT
(5 gallons)

Ingredients:

7 lb.	**Pale malt**	**3.2 kilo**
4 oz.	**Hops**	**110 g.**
3 lb.	**Demerara sugar (as syrup)**	**1.4 kilo**
½ lb.	**Brown malt**	**230 g.**
12½ oz.	**Crystal malt**	**375 g.**
2 oz.	**Black malt**	**55 g.**
3 oz.	**Chocolate malt**	**90 g.**
	Beer yeast	

Method:

Crush and mash all the grains at a temperature of 63°C. (146°F.) for an hour, then drop to 57–60°C. (138–140°F.), until mash runs clear. Strain off, add syrup and hops and boil gently for 30 minutes. When temperature drops to 15°C. (60°F.), add activated yeast and ferment out. Bottle and keep for at least eight weeks before opening.

OATMEAL STOUT (1)

Ingredients:

¾ lb.	Rye	350 g.
½ lb.	Black malt	225 g.
½ lb.	Pale malt	225 g.
2 teaspoons	Brewing yeast and nutrient	
6 oz.	Oatmeal	165 g.
2 oz.	Hops	55 g.
4 lb.	Sugar	2 kilo
½ teaspoon	Citric acid	
4 gallons	Water (soft)	18 litres

Method:

Bring two gallons of water up to 150°F. in a boiler. Pour most of this into a polythene 2-gallon bucket, and then sprinkle in the malts, rye and oatmeal. Insert a 50-watt immersion heater and switch on; cover bucket closely with blanket and wrap it to conserve heat. Keep the heater on for eight hours, holding the temperature at between 62°C. and 68°C. (145°F. and 155°F.). Then strain the wort back into the boiler, add 1½ oz. of hops and the salt, bring to the boil and simmer for 40 minutes. Add the remaining ½ oz. of hops and simmer for five minutes. Put the 4 lb. sugar and the citric acid into a brewbin and strain the wort on to them. Stir thoroughly, bring the total volume up to four gallons by adding the remainder of the water, cold, and stir again.

Ferment and continue as usual.

CHAPTER 12

Malt Extract
Beers

Malt extract beers may be made from a whole range of extracts which are not necessarily hopped, as are those in most kits, thus giving the brewer greater economy and the chance of selecting his own hops and adjuncts.

The extract is dissolved in hot water and boiled with the hops and any malt or grits included in order improve or change the flavour. Any remaining water can be added cold.

Extract beers are more economical, of course, and the whole range of beers and stouts is still within your grasp. The big advantages are (a) cheapness and (b) the avoidance of mashing and sparging necessary when brewing from grain malt, but there is a slight sacrifice of quality compared with mashed beers, in most home brewers' opinion.

Malt extract varies greatly in quality and specification so it pays to be careful what you buy. Chemists sell ordinary (unhopped) malt extract usually in 1 lb. or 2 lb. glass jars—avoid that flavoured with cod liver oil for obvious reasons!—but the best brewing extract is usually sold in 2 lb. or 4 lb. tins; it is naturally cheaper if purchased in bulk, in 7 lb. or 14 lb. plastic tubs or in even bigger quantity.

It is good policy to buy a diastatic extract, i.e. one which has the power of converting the starch in any other grain used in the brew to fermentable sugar; Edme's DMS and Superflavex are examples.

Check whether or not it is already hopped; unhopped extract is usually cheaper.

The best brewing grades have the right balance for the production of body and alcohol, the right protein balance for good clearing and head retention, freedom from bacterial infection which could cause off flavours, and a standardised low colour, so that you can "tint up" to your own requirements with roasted malts or caramel.

The big disadvantage of beers made entirely from extract is that they sometimes have a characteristic nutty flavour which is quite distinctive. Some do not find it disagreeable, but if you do, it can be minimised by using, say, 1 lb. of crystal malt or 1 lb. of roasted barley. This should be cracked with a mincer and boiled with the hops. Or you can use 1 lb. of unmalted whole barley in each 4 or 5 gallons. Soak the barley in water for two or three days, pressure cook for 30 minutes in three pints of water (or boil till grains split) and then boil this barley mash with the hops and extract.

If one wishes to economise, household sugar can be substituted for some of the malt, and one can thus obtain varying strengths of flavour and varying alcoholic strengths. A good rule of thumb is that $1\frac{1}{2}$–2 lb. (500 g.–1 kilo) of "sugar" (i.e. the combined weight of extract and sugar) per gallon will give an exceedingly strong beer, and below 1 lb. (500 g.) per gallon will produce weaker beers.

So all you need to remember is that the *total* sugar can range anywhere between 1 lb. and 2 lb. per gallon, counting extract and household sugar pound for pound. But do not fall into the trap, for reasons of false economy, of using a high proportion of sucrose, or the quality of the beer will suffer.

From the following table, which was devised a few years ago by Mr. Humfrey Wakefield and since used successfully by thousands of brewers all over the world, you can compile your own recipes to obtain exactly the brew you require.

Those who want a light beer for summer drinking in quantity will prefer No. 1, those who want an "ordinary" bitter strength will choose No. 2, those who want "best bitter" strength No. 3, and those who want really strong beer of "barley wine" strength No. 4. The stronger the beer, the less it can be drunk in quantity and, of course, the more expensive it is to make. Most home brewers will come to prefer the strength of Nos. 2 and 3.

To make Five Gallons

Recipe	1	2	3	4
Alcohol	3%	5%	7%	9%
Gravity at Start ...	30	45	60	80
Gravity at Finish ...	-2	0	5	9
Gallons Water ...	5	5	5	5
Sugar (pounds) ...	3	4	5	6
Malt Extract (pounds)	1	2	3	4
Hops	$1\frac{1}{2}$ oz.	2 oz.	4–6 oz.	6–8 oz.
Price per pint ...	3p	4p	5p	6p
Days to clear ...	7	14	21	28
Keeps for	Weeks	Months	Months	Years

Use also in each case: 1 pkt. Dried Brewer's Yeast.
Water treatment as necessary.
A good pinch of citric acid.

For Stout: Boil up $\frac{1}{2}$ lb. patent black malt grains and 4 oz. flaked barley with the hops, in Recipe 3 or 4.

THE PROCEDURE

Malt extract, as already pointed out, is the easiest ingredient to use because excellent results can be obtained from a "cold brew", i.e. one where it is unnecessary to boil the whole of the wort. Most experienced brewers, however, *do* prefer to boil the whole wort to ensure its complete sterility, and to achieve clarity, as already explained, and if you have a large enough boiler there is no reason why all the ingredients should not be put in it and boiled together.

If your local water is *soft*, you will probably succeed best with milds, browns and stouts, but if you wish to make a good pale ale or bitter it will help if you add one teaspoon of plaster of paris per gallon of water. If your local water is *hard*, you will do best to make bitter or pale ale, and will find it an advantage to boil *all* the water rather than to use the cold brew method. The addition of a little salt also helps.

Otherwise bring to the boil as much water as your boiler will take, say two or three gallons (after room has been left for the hops and the vigour of the boiling). Add the malt extract, hops, water treatment, and colouring. You can darken the colour of a beer by using caramel colouring (Crosse & Blackwell gravy browning is useful, for it is only caramel, as you will see from the label) or by including some of the heavily roasted malts (this is how stouts get their colour). The darker the malt the more it contributes by way of colour and the less to the strength.

Boil for at least 45 minutes; add a few extra hops in the last five minutes to restore aroma lost in boiling. Pour this wort into the fermenting vessel and make up with cold or warm water to the required final volume, and add a pinch of citric acid to ensure a quick start to fermentation. Leave enough room for the frothing which will take place. Allow to cool to 21°C. (70°F.) and then add yeast and nutrient.

WITH ADDED MALT AND GRITS

Remember that if you are using grain malt or other grits to support your extract, and to improve the flavour (rather than just for colouring), you will need to follow a slightly different procedure, for in this case you will need to observe the mashing principles for grain malt beers if you are to obtain the maximum value from your grain.

In this case put the grain, the extract and any water treatment being used into about half the water, say 1½ gallons, raise temperature to 150°F, and hold it closely to this temperature for about three-quarters of an hour.

Then add the hops, boil for half an hour, and strain on to any additional sugar, before making up to the required quantity with more water. Pale and crystal malts should be cracked, heavily roasted malts used whole.

When the wort has cooled to 15°C. the yeast is pitched, and the fermentation, racking, fining and bottling carried out in the usual way.

If using an open bin, cover with a thick cloth, and rest the lid on top. The first "head" of froth which forms on the brew evidently carries up with it much of the aromatic oils of the hops, for if you taste it you will see that it has a pronounced bitterness that lingers unpleasantly in the back of the throat, and your beer may later have this quality, a stronger bitterness than the one we seek, and tasted further back in the throat. So skim it off. If you are reluctant to throw away the skimmed foam (and it does seem a shame) leave it on the brew, but in that case cut down drastically on the hops.

If, despite your precautions, you eventually produce a beer which is too bitter for your taste, the bitterness can be masked by the use of liquorice. Dissolve a 3p stick in a saucepan over the stove, with a little hot water, and add the resulting syrup to your brew "to taste", that is, a little at a time, until it seems to you that it has done the trick.

With a "closed" fermentation and a "bottom" yeast (one which works from the bottom) further skimming is unnecessary. After the initial frothing and the formation of the exciting "corona", or ring, the "head" may turn a dirty brown. Do not worry about this; all is in order.

With strong beers, add half the sugar at the outset, the remainder after three days, stirring thoroughly; if all the sugar is used at the outset they may "stick" at 1020 or so.

When the surface of the beer begins to clear, but bubbles collect in a ring in the centre (or when the S.G. is below 1010, and as near as possible to 1000) you can bottle.

Many of the best recipes for this brewing method were devised by Dave Line and were published in "The Amateur Winemaker and Brewer" magazine and in his excellent book "Beer Kits and Brewing". Here are several of them which have not been published elsewhere, together with many of my own formulations as a guide to your experiments.

5 STAR BITTER
(5 gallons, 25 litres)

Ingredients:

4 lb.	**Tin malt extract**	**1.8 kg.**
1 lb.	**White sugar**	**450 gm.**
1 lb.	**Golden syrup**	**450 gm.**
4 oz.	**Hops (Goldings if named)**	**110 gm.**
	Sachet of brewing yeast	
	10 saccharin tablets	
	Gelatine finings	

Method:
1. Open the tins of extract and golden syrup and stand them in hot water for a few minutes to make them flow more easily.
2. Pour the extract into the saucepan and add as much water as possible. Leave at least 2 inches of freeboard to accommodate the sticky foam that forms during boiling.
3. Boil and then simmer the extract for 15 minutes and then switch

off. Add and stir in the hops. Repeat the stirring two or three more times over the next ten minutes.

4. Using a colander or large sieve, strain off the liquid wort from the hops into the fermentation bin. Rinse out the remaining absorbed extract from the hops with a couple of kettlefulls of hot water.
5. Dissolve the golden syrup and sugar in hot water and add this to the wort as well. Top up the bin to the 5 gallon mark with cold water.
6. Add the yeast, saccharin tablets and finings, replace the lid and store the bin in a warm place (around 70°F.) for the fermentation to start.
7. The yeast will start to form a thick frothy foam over the surface as fermentation progresses. Skim off any dirty scum that forms and stir daily until the activity diminishes and the beer starts to clear at the surface. Usually fermentation is complete after 5 or 6 days.
8. Prime and bottle.

BREWSTER BITTER
(5 gallons, Original Gravity 1039, 25 litres)

Ingredients:

4 lb.	**D.M.S., Boots or Muntona Medium Malt extract**	**2 kg.**
4 oz.	**Crushed crystal malt**	**125 gm.**
2 oz.	**Crushed wheat malt**	**60 gm.**
2 lb.	**White sugar**	**1 kg.**
2 oz.	**Goldings hops**	**60 gm.**
1 oz.	**Hallertau hops**	**30 gm.**
	Sachet of beer yeast	
	Pale ale/Bitter water treatment Salts	

Method:

Boil the malt extract with the hops for 45 minutes. Pitch in the crushed grain for the last five minutes.

Meanwhile:

Dissolve the sugar in boiling water and pour into a sterilised fermenting bin. Also make up a yeast starter with a little cooled wort solution.

Then:

Switch off the boiler and allow the cooked wort to stand for five minutes. Strain off as much of the clear liquid as possible into the fermenting bin. Add a kettleful of hot water to the redundant solids in the boiling pan and allow to stand again. Straining off this time should retrieve most of the absorbed extract.

Top the fermenting bin up to the final quantity with cold water and allow to cool to room temperature before pitching in the yeast starter. Ferment 4–8 days until the S.G. falls to around 1006. Remove surface scum on the brew and drop in two crushed Campden tablets. Snap on the lid and leave two days undisturbed.

Bottle or cask as appropriate, priming at the rate of $\frac{1}{2}$ teaspoon/pint (5 ml./lit.) or $\frac{1}{2}$ oz./gal. (3 gm./lit.).

Sample casked beer after 10 days and bottled brews after three weeks.

MARKSMAN BITTER
5 gallons (25 litres)

Ingredients:

4 lb.	Malt extract	2000 gm.
3 lb.	Crushed pale malt	1500 gm.
5 oz.	Flaked maize	150 gm.
2 teaspoons	Brewers caramel	10 ml.
1 lb.	Glucose chips	500 gm.
2 oz.	Goldings hops	60 gm.
1 oz. approx.	Styrian Goldings isomerised hop extract	30 gm. approx
	Few drops of hop oil essence	
$\frac{1}{2}$ oz.	Dried brewers yeast	15 gm.
$\frac{1}{2}$ oz.	Davis gelatine	15 gm.
	Pale ale water treatment	

Method:

1. Add the water treatment to 1 gallon of water and raise its temperature to around 60°C. (140°F.). Add the crushed malt grains and flakes. Stir continuously and raise the temperature to 67°C. 155°F. before switching off the heat. Maintain the temperature as close to 65°C. (150°F.) for two hours. Strain off the sweet wort and rinse the grains to collect 3 gallons (15 litres) of wort.

2. Boil the wort with the Goldings hops for one hour and then strain off into the fermenting vessel.
3. Boil the malt extract, glucose chips and caramel in sufficient water for a few minutes and add this to the fermenting bin as well. Top up the bin to the final quantity with cold water. When cool to room temperature pitch in the yeast and hop extract.
4. Ferment four to five days or as necessary for the S.G. to fall to 1,008 and rack the brew into a 25 litre polythene cube
5. "Rest" the beer for a week, fine with gelatine.
6. Rack into pressure barrel and prime with 1½ oz. (45 gm.) of sugar.

SPARTAN BITTER
(40 pints)
Cost approximately: Less than 4p per pint.
Strength: 3.7%

Ingredients:

2 lb.	**Boots malt extract**	**1 kilo**
2 lb.	**Demerara sugar**	**1 kilo**
5	**Saccharin tablets**	
2 oz.	**Hops (Goldings or Fuggles)**	**55 g.**
1 sachet	**Boots beer yeast**	

Method:
1. Boil the malt extract in a gallon or so of water for 45 minutes. Include any crushed grain, caramel or whole hops in the boil as well.
2. Strain off into a fermenting bin and add the saccharin tablets and hop extract as required. Also stir in the golden syrup or sugar (previously dissolved in a little boiling water) before topping up the bin to the final quantity with cold water.
3. Add the yeast when cool and ferment for 3–4 days.
4. Rack off into gallon jars or a polythene cube fitted with an airlock and leave the beer to clear. Gelatine finings may be used to hasten the clarification.
5. When clear, siphon off into primed beer bottle or a pressure barrel and leave one week before sampling.

BARLEY MOW BITTER (Draught)
5 gallons O.G.35

Ingredients:

2 lb.	Malt extract	1 kg.
2 lb.	Barley syrup	1 kg.
2 lb.	Golden syrup	1 kg.
4 oz.	Goldings hops	100 g.
	Irish Moss preparation	
	Beer yeast	
	Gelatine finings	

Method:

1. Boil the malt extract, barley or maize syrup, and Irish moss in two gallons of water for 20 minutes. Then switch off.
2. Stir in the hops and stir occasionally over the next ten minutes.
3. Strain off the wort from the hops into a fermentation vessel.
4. Dissolve the Golden syrup, sugar or molasses as appropriate in hot water and add this to the bin as well. Top up the bin to the 5 gallon mark with cold water.
5. When cool to 70°F. add the yeast and saccharin tablets if used and ferment in a warm place for 4–5 days. Skim off any dirty yeast.
6. Rack off into a polythene cube or gallon jars and add gelatine finings. Leave two days to clear.
7. Rack off again into a 5 gallon pressure barrel. Add two dessertspoonfuls of sugar or preferably golden syrup for priming. Fit an injector unit or plain cap as preferred.
8. Sample for clarity and condition after one week.

More 4-gallon (18 litre) formulations worth trying:

BITTER (1)

2 lb.	Malt extract	1 kilo
2 lb.	White sugar	1 kilo
3 oz.	Boots hops	85 g.
1 dsrtspoon	Caramel colouring	
4 gallons	Water (hard)	18 litres
$\frac{1}{2}$ teaspoon	Citric acid	5 g.
2 teaspoons	Dried beer yeast	

BITTER (2)

4 lb.	C.A. malt extract	1.8 kilo
8 dsrtspoons	Medium dark dried malt extract	80 ml.
4 oz.	Hops	100 g.
1½ lb.	Granulated sugar	675 g.
4 gallons	Water (hard)	18 litres
	Brewing yeast	

BITTER (3)

6 lb.	Malt extract	2.5 kilo
3 lb.	Pale malt	1.25 kilo
3 lb.	Sugar	1.25 kilo
6 oz.	Golding hops	150 g.
4 gallons	Water (hard)	18 litres
	Brewer's yeast	

BERRY BREW (Best Bitter)

(5 gallons/20 litres)

4 lb.	Malt extract	1.8 kilo
4 lb.	Sugar	1.8 kilo
1 teaspoon (level)	Citric acid	5 g.
2 teaspoons (level)	Salt	10 g.
5 gallons	Water	20 litres
4 oz.	Hops	100 g.
1dsrtspoon	Caramel	10 mls.
	(Crosse & Blackwells gravy browning) boiled with hops	
	Brewers' yeast	

DRAUGHT PALE ALE
O.G.37

Ingredients:

3 lb.	Malt extract	1.5 kg.
1 lb.	Maize syrup	500 gm.
2 lb.	Demerara sugar	1 kg.
4 oz.	Goldings hops	100 g.
	Irish moss preparation	
	Beer yeast	
	Gelatine finings	

Method:
As for Barley Mow Bitter.

"LANCASTER" LIGHT ALE
32 pints (20 litres)
Cost approximately: 4½p per pint
Strength: 3.4%

Ingredients:

2 lb.	Edme D.M.S. malt extract	1 kilo
1 lb.	Soft dark brown sugar	450 g.
1 tub	Inn Sign hop extract	
1 sachet	Edme beer yeast	

Method:
As for Spartan Bitter.

FALLBRIGHT LIGHT ALE
32 pints (20 litres)

Ingredients:

3.3 lb.	Mutona Medium malt extract	1½ kg.
4 oz.	Crushed crystal malt	125 gm.
1 lb.	Invert sugar	500 gm.
1 teaspoon	Yeast nutrient	5 ml.
2 oz.	Golding hops	60 gm.
	Heading liquid/powder	
	Beer yeast	

Method:

Dissolve the malt extract in two gallons of hot water. Add the crushed malt and hops and boil the mixture for 45 minutes. Strain off the solids and add the glucose to the hot liquid. Top up to the final quantity with cold water. When cool pitch in the beer yeast and ferment four to five days. On the third day add a requisite dose of heading agent. When the fermentation has almost stopped, add a dessertspoonful of sugar and leave for one more day before bottling in primed beer bottles.

Other formulations for 4 gallons (18 litres) of LIGHT ALE:

LIGHT ALE (1)

6 lb.	Malt extract	2.5 kilo
2 lb.	Barley	1 kilo
1 dsrtspoon	Caramel	10 ml.
3 oz.	Hallertauer hops	85 g.
4 gallons	Water (hard)	18 litres
½ teaspoon	Citric acid	5 g.
	Lager yeast	

LIGHT ALE (2).

5 lb.	Malt extract (DMS)	2 kilo
2 lb.	Pale malt	1 kilo
1 lb.	Flaked barley	450 g.
1 lb.	Brewing sugar	450 g.
4 oz.	Golding hops	100 g.
4 gallons	Water (hard)	18 litres
	Beer yeast	

MALTHOUSE MILD
5 gallons O.G. 33

Ingredients:

2 lb.	Malt extract	1 kilo
2 lb.	Barley syrup	1 kilo
1½ lb.	Soft brown sugar	675 g
1 tblespoon	Molasses	
3 oz.	Crushed black malt	85 g.
2 oz.	Fuggles hops	50 g.
10	Saccharin tablets	
	Irish moss preparation	
	Beer yeast	
	Gelatine finings	

Method:

As Barley Mow Bitter.

BLACKMOOR MILD ALE
5 gallons (25 litres)

Ingredients:

4 lb.	D.M.S. malt extract	2000 gm.
2 lb.	White sugar	1000 gm.
2 oz.	Crushed black malt	60 gm.
3 teaspoons	Brewers caramel	15 ml.
2 oz. (approx.)	Hop extract	60 gm. (approx.)
½ oz.	Dried brewers yeast	15 gm.

Method:

Boil the malt extract, black malt and hop extract for 30 minutes in 2 gallons (9 litres) of water and strain off into the fermenting bin. Dissolve the sugar and caramel in boiling water and add this as well. Top up the bin to the final quantity with cold water. When cool to room temperature pitch in the yeast and ferment four to five days before racking into a primed pressure barrel or polythene cube.

MILD (draught)
4 gallons (18 litres)

4 lb.	C.A. malt extract	1.8 kilo
2 lb.	Crystal malt	900 g.
4 gallons	Water (soft)	18 litres
	Brewer's yeast	
1 lb.	Pale malt	450 g.
1½ lb.	Glucose chippings	675 g.
4 oz.	Fuggles hops	100 g.

Method:

General boiling-up method as Blackmoor Mild Ale.

NUT BROWN ALE
5 gallons (25 litres)

4 lb.	S.F.X. malt extract	2000 gm.
3 oz.	Crushed chocolate malt	100 gm.
1 lb.	Light brown sugar	500 gm.
2 oz.	Northern Brewer isomerised hop extract	60 gm. (equiv.)
½ oz.	Fresh Northern Brewer or Northdown hops	15 gm.
1 sachet	Dried beer yeast	1
10	Saccharin tablets	10
	Heading liquid	

Method:

Boil the malt extract, chocolate malt and fresh hops for 30 minutes in 2–4 gallons of water. Strain off the solids into a fermenting bin. Top up to the final volume with cold water. When cool add the hop extract, saccharin and yeast. Ferment 4–6 days as required, rack off and allow to settle under airlock protection for a few days before bottling in primed bottles to which one drop of heading liquid per pint of capacity has been added. Sample after two weeks.

BROWN ALE (1)

4 lb.	C.A. malt extract	1.8 kilo
1½ lb.	Medium dark dried malt extract	675 g.
½ lb.	Sugar	225 g.
4 gallons	Water (soft)	18 litres
	Beer yeast	
½ lb.	Black malt	225 g.
½ oz.	Crystal malt	15 g.
1⅛ oz.	Fuggles hops	45 g.
1 lb.	Lactose (dissolved in ½ pint (280 ml.)	450 g.
	boiling water and added before bottling	

BROWN ALE (2)

2 lb.	Malt extract	1 kilo
4 lb.	Brown sugar	1.5 kilo
8 oz.	Black malt	225 g.
1½ oz.	Fuggles hops	45 g.
½ teaspoon	Salt	2.5 ml.
4 gallons	Water (soft)	18 litres
	Brewer's yeast	

SWEET BROWN ALE (3)

2 lb.	Malt extract	1 kilo
4 lb.	Dark Sugar	1.5 kilo
2 oz.	Hops	50 g.
2 teaspoons	Yeast	10 ml.
16 oz.	Lactose	500 g.
	Water to 4 gallons (soft)	18 litres
8 oz.	Black malt grains	225 g.

N.B.—The lactose is dissolved in half a pint of boiling water, cooled, and added to the ale before bottling (i.e. 1 oz. to each quart flagon).

BUCKINGHAM BROWN ALE
5 gallons (20 litres)
Cost approximately: Just over 4p per pint
Strength: 3.8%

Ingredients:

2 lb.	Boots malt extract	1 kilo
½ lb.	Crushed crystal malt	500 g.
4 teaspoons	Brewers caramel	15 ml.
2 lb.	White sugar	1 kilo
8	Saccharin tablets	
1 tub	Inn Sign hop extract	
1 sachet	Boots beer yeast	

Method:

As Spartan Bitter

BURTON BROWN ALE
3 gallons (15 litres)

Ingredients:

2 lb.	Edme S.F.X.	907 gm.
3 oz.	Crushed black malt	100 gm.
1 lb.	Glucose powder (or chips)	500 gm.
1 oz.	Hops	30 gm.
	Heading liquid/powder	
	Sweetex liquid	
	Beer yeast	

Method:

As for Fallbright Light Ale except that 24 drops of Sweetex are added with the heading liquid.

Other recommended formulations to make 4 gallons (18 litres):

DARK BROWN ALE (4)

2 lb.	Malt extract	
2 oz.	Hops	
4 sticks	Liquorice, boiled	
4 lb.	Brown sugar	1.8 kilo
	Water to 4 gallons (soft)	18 litres
	Stout yeast	

STRONG BROWN ALE (5)

½ lb.	Milled black malt		
3½ lb.	Malt extract		
4 lb.	Brown sugar		
4 oz.	Fuggles hops		
½ teaspoon	Citric acid	2.5 g.	
	Water to 4 gallons (soft)	18 litres	
	Brewers' yeast		

STAR STOUT (SWEET)
5 gallons (25 litres)

Ingredients:

5 lb.	D.M.S. malt extract	2500 gm.
1 lb.	Crushed chocolate malt	500 gm.
2 lb.	Demerara sugar	1000 gm.
15	Saccharin tablets	
2 oz.	Fuggles hops	60 gm.
1 oz.	W.G.V. isomerised hop extract	30 gm.
(approx.)		(approx.)
½ oz.	Dried beer yeast	15 gm.

Method:

Boil the malt extract, crushed grain and whole hops in 2 gallons (10 litres) of water for 45 minutes. Strain off into a fermenting bin and stir in the quota of sugar and hop extract. Top up to the final quantity with cold water before sprinkling in the beer yeast. Ferment until the S.G. falls to 1,004 and bottle in primed beer bottles. Mature for 10 days before sampling.

EXTRA STOUT (DRY)
5 gallons (25 litres)

Ingredients:

5 lb.	**D.M.S. malt extract**	**2500 gm.**
1 lb.	**Crushed roast barley**	**500 gm.**
2 lb.	**White sugar**	**1000 gm.**
2 oz.	**Northern Brewer hops**	**60 gm.**
2 oz.	**Bullion isomerised hop extract**	**60 gm.**
(approx.)		**(approx.)**
½ oz.	**Dried beer yeast**	**(15 gm.)**

Method:

As Star Stout.

BLACK BARREL STOUT
4 gallons (18 litres) with O.G.45

4 lb.	**Malt extract**	**2 kilo**
1 lb.	**Crushed crystal malt**	**500 g.**
½ lb.	**Crushed patent black malt**	**250 g.**
2 lb.	**Golden syrup**	**1 kilo**
20	**Saccharin tablets**	
2 oz.	**Hops**	**50 g.**
	Brewing yeast	

Method:

Boil the malt extract, hops and grain (if required) in two gallons (9 litres) of water for 45 minutes. Strain off into fermenting bin and rinse with another ½ gallon (2 litres) of hot water. Dissolve the Golden syrup in a few pints of hot water and add this to the bin as well. Top up to the required gallonage with cold water and when the wort is cool add the yeast and saccharin tablets.

Ferment for four to five days and then rack off and fine with gelatine before casking or bottling the beer as required.

Other recommended formulations to make 4 gallons (18 litres):

PORTER

2 lb.	Malt extract	1 kilo
1 lb.	Patent black malt	450 g.
1 lb.	Flaked barley	450 g.
2 lb.	White sugar	900 g.
4 gallons	Water (soft)	18 litres
3 oz.	Fuggles hops	85 g.
	Brewers' yeast	

STOUT

2 lb.	Malt extract	1 kilo
$\frac{1}{2}$ lb.	Pale malt	225 g.
1 lb.	Patent black malt	450 g.
	boiled with 3 oz. hops for 30 mins.	
3 lb.	Dark brown sugar	1.3 kilo
1 teaspoon	Salt	5 g
	Water to 4 gallons (soft)	18 litres
	Stout yeast	

OATMEAL STOUT

6 lb.	Malt extract	2.7 kilo
1 lb.	Black malt	450 g.
2 lb.	Oatmeal	900 g.
4 lb.	Sugar	1.8 kilo
8 oz.	Lactose	225 g.
6 oz.	Fuggles hops	150 g.
4 gallons	Water (soft)	18 litres
	Cultured stout yeast	

Dissolve lactose in half pint of boiling water, cool, and add before bottling.

DOUBLE STOUT (Good for you!)

5½ lb.	DMS malt extract	2.5 kilo
1 lb.	Black malt, cracked	450 g.
12 oz.	Flaked barley	300 g.
2 teaspoons	Salt (level)	10 g.
4½ gallons	Water (soft)	20 litres
4 oz.	Fuggles hops	100 g.
	Cultured stout yeast	

LAGER

Malt extract is not really well suited to the production of lager since when using it it is difficult to obtain the authentic light colour usually expected in a lager, but here are some recipes which give reasonably good results.

The critical factors in producing quality lager are a low fermenting temperature from start to finish, (at no time above 18°C. (65°F.) and preferably not above 16°C. The fermentation should be under air lock, and a true lager *bottom*-fermenting yeast be chosen. The beer should be rested, on the lees, for at least a month at a temperature of about 45°F. and then be siphoned off and primed as usual.

TROJAN LAGER
5 gallons (22 litres) strength 3.2%
(Cost, about 3½p per pint)

Ingredients:

2 lb.	D.M.S. malt extract
2 lb.	Golden Syrup
5	Saccharin tablets
2 oz.	Hallertau hops
1 sachet	Lager yeast

Method:

As for Spartan Bitter.

136

Other useful formulations are:

LIGHT LAGER
4 gallons (18 litres)

3½ lb.	Malt extract	1.5 kilo
2 oz.	Hallertauer hops	55 g.
	Lager yeast	
4 gallons	Water (soft)	18 litres
½ teaspoon	Citric acid	5 g.

LAGER
4 gallons (18 litres)

5 lb.	Malt extract (DMS)	2 kilo
4 lb.	Pale malt	1.8 kilo
4 lb.	Sugar	1.5 kilo
4 oz.	Saaz hops	100 g.
4 gallons	Water (soft)	18 litres
	Lager yeast	

CANADIAN LAGER

This recipe is for a lager specially suited to the Canadian palate:

Ingredients:

5	Imperial gallons of water	
2½ lb.	Tin of light barley malt extract	1 kilo
½ oz.	Kent finishing hops	15 g.
2 oz.	Bramling or Cluster hops	50 g.
4 lb.	Corn sugar (Dextrose)	2 kilo
1 teaspoon	Citric acid	
2–3 teaspoons	Salt	
½ teaspoon	Yeast energiser	
½ teaspoon	Special beer finings	
1 teaspoon	Heading liquid	
	Lager yeast	

Method:

Be sure to save two full cups of corn sugar for bottling; then make sure your yeast starter is ready to use. Boil as much of the water as possible. Naturally, this will depend on the size of the container you have, but not less than one gallon. Along with the water you should boil the malt extract, 2 ozs. of hops (broken up and tied in cheese-cloth), the salt and citric acid. Simmer very gently for 1–2 hours with a lid on to reduce evaporation. As you remove this from the heat, add the $\frac{1}{2}$ oz. of Kent hops which can remain in the "wort" during the primary fermentation. Pour this hot wort over the corn sugar (minus the two cups, remember). Stir to dissolve the sugar and add the balance of the water to make up a total of five Imperial gallons.

Cover the "wort" with a sheet of plastic tied down and allow the mixture to cool to around 15°C. (60°F.). This may take up to 12 hours, so don't hold your breath. The fermentation vessel should be in a place where the temperature will remain between 12°C. and 22°C. (55°F. and 65°F.). When the "wort" is cool, take a Specific Gravity reading to make sure it is between 33 and 38. (The starting gravity should be 30 to 40, and the beer should finish at 0, i.e., 1.035 to 1.000). If it is not correct, you can adjust it by adding more sugar or water, depending on whether it is high or low.

Now add the active lager yeast and cover once again with the plastic sheet. After about four or five days of active ferment you can stark checking the Specific Gravity to see how the ferment is progressing. It will probably take six to ten days to get down to between 5 to 10 (1.010) depending on the temperature. When it gets to this point, skim off the floating hops, add the yeast energiser, and siphon the wort into the carboy. Don't fill the carboy too full because you need room to add the "finings" at this point. Dissolve the half teaspoon of finings in one cup of very hot water (not boiling) and pour this on top of the beer in the carboy and stir in thoroughly with the handle end of your wooden spoon. The carboy should now be filled to within two or three inches of the fermentation lock which should be properly attached at this time.

Now that your beer is in the carboy with the fermentation lock attached and placed in a cool (55°–65°F.), place away from the light, it is safe even if you don't get to look at it for up to three weeks. Under normal circumstances, it will be clear and the gravity down to zero (1.000) in about ten days. Don't worry about the extra time involved in making beer this way, inasmuch as your beer is ageing in the carboy and will be ready that much sooner after bottling. In any case, when these two things occur, i.e., the brew is reasonably clear and the gravity is down to 1.000, the time has come for bottling.

Now take those two cups of sugar saved from your 4 lb. (2 kilo). Siphon off about two pints of beer into a clean saucepan, warm on the stove, and dissolve the two cups of sugar to make a beer sugar syrup. Be sure the saucepan is big enough, because the mixture will foam all over the stove if it's not, and annoy your wife somewhat. When this is ready, siphon off the rest of the beer into your clean primary fermenter, being careful not to disturb the yeast sediment.

Save your yeast. At this time you can get your yeast back for your next brew by swirling the sediment in the bottom of the carboy and, using a small funnel, pour it into a clean beer bottle and cap immediately. Place this bottle in the crisper part of your refrigerator where it won't freeze. The next time you make beer you will not have to grow your yeast but merely take this bottle from the refrigerator open it and add it to the "wort" when the wort is properly cooled. This yeast starter will be good in the refrigerator for approximately three to five weeks in the case of Lager yeast and two to three weeks for Ale yeast.

Now that we have the clear beer in the primary fermenter and the gravity is 1.000, stir in the syrup, making sure it is thoroughly distributed, but do not aerate the beer too much. At the same time you can be stirring in the teaspoonful of Heading Liquid. The gravity of this mixture should be approximately 1.005. We will assume that you have already prepared your five dozen bottles, that they are thoroughly clean and standing in a convenient place to be filled to within one inch of the cap. It does not matter if they are wet inside, in fact, it may make it easier to fill them by reducing the foaming. Cap them immediately and place in a temperature of 15–20°C. (60–70°F.) for ten days and then chill and try the results of your labour.

For Ale use the same recipe with the addition of 1 oz. (30 g.) of Gypsum, and Ale instead of Lager beer yeast.

Before it has completely worked out, it is important to move the lager into a carboy and attach a fermentation lock, not gallon jugs but glass or plastic carboys. It should be Lagered at a temperature of around 45°–50°F., or lower, for at least one month, then carefully siphoned off the lees and 12 oz. of corn sugar added to five gallons, plus a teaspoon of heading liquid and a teaspoon of ascorbic acid. Then of course it is essential, as all Canadian beer is normally bottled and crown capped, that the same procedure be followed here. It should stand in the bottle for at least three weeks to a month and is not likely to be at its peak much before three months from the outset of fermentation.

PATRIARCH PILSENER

Ingredients:

2 tins	(2½ lb. each) Light malt extract	2 kilo
2 oz.	Brewer's gold or cluster hops	55 g.
¼ oz.	Kent Finishing hops	10 g.
4 lb.	Corn sugar	2 kilo
5	Imperial gallons of water	22 litres
2 teaspoons	Salt	
1 teaspoon	Citric acid	
1 teaspoon	Heading liquid	
½ teaspoon	Beer finings	
½ teaspoon	Grape tannin	
	Lager yeast (dry or liquid)	
	Starting gravity: 43 to 45	
	Terminal gravity: 1.003	

The method is the same as for Canadian Light Lager.

DRIED MALT EXTRACT

The dried powder malt extract on the market is rather pleasanter to handle than the sticky, liquid variety, although a little more expensive.

In each of these German recipes, boil the dried malt and hops in the water for half an hour. Strain into fermentation jar or jars to take two gallons, cool to 70°F., add yeast and nutrient, fit air lock and leave to ferment in warm room for seven to eight days. "Prime" as directed under that heading, and bottle.

Light Lager: 2½ lb. dried malt extract, 2 oz. hops, 2 gallons of water, beer yeast.

Lager (Pilsener style): 4½ lb. dried malt extract, 1 oz. hops, 2 gallons water, beer yeast.

Lager: (Munich style): 5 lb. dried malt extract, ½ oz. of caramel, 1 oz. hops, 4 gallons water, beer yeast.

Dark Beer or Porter: 6½ lb. dried malt extract, 1 oz. of caramel, 3 gallons water, beer yeast.

Ale: 6½ lb. dried malt extract, 3 gallons water, 2 oz. hops, beer yeast.

CHAPTER 13

Novelty Beers

True beer, of course, is that made from malt and hops, but there are many other "beers", many of them delightful drinks in their own right, and some of them of undoubted therapeutic value. It is fun to experiment with them, and to produce unusual drinks which can NOT be purchased at the local.

APPLE ALE

Here is a very old recipe for a cider-like ale:

Ingredients:

3 lb.	Apples (windfalls will do)	1.5 kilo
1 oz.	Root ginger	30 g.
½ teaspoon	Cloves	
½ teaspoon	Cinnamon	
1½ lb.	White sugar	675 g.
1 gallon	Water	4.5 litres
	Yeast and nutrient	

Method:

Wash the apples, cutting out any damaged portions, and grate or mince. Add the water, cold, and the yeast and nutrient, cover with a thick cloth, and leave in a warm room for a week, stirring thoroughly daily. Strain on to the sugar, bruised ginger, cloves and cinnamon, and press out as much extra juice from the pulp as possible by squeezing it in a cloth. Stir vigorously, cover and leave for about five days. Strain into screw-stoppered flagons. Store in a cool place and the ale will be ready to drink after about another fortnight.

BRAHN ALE!

Ingredients:

1 lb.	**Bran**	**450 g.**
2 oz.	**Hops**	**55 g.**
2 lb.	**Demerara sugar**	**1 kilo**
	Gravy browning	
	Yeast and nutrient	
3 gallons	**Water**	**13.5 litres**

Method:

Put two gallons of water in a 3-gallon boiler, and put third gallon by. Bring to boil. Add sugar, hops, bran, and 2 teaspoonsful of gravy browning (the liquid variety—which is only caramel colouring). Boil gently for $1\frac{1}{2}$ hours. Strain through muslin into crock and on to third gallon of cold water. Leave to cool until blood heat, then pour into three 1-gallon jars, filling to shoulder only. Add brewer's yeast, if obtainable, or dried yeast, fit traps and leave for seven days (in room temperature. Then siphon into strong beer bottles and cork or seal really tightly. The beer may be drunk after another week, but will not be really clear. To clarify, it should be kept at least three weeks after bottling in **a cool place.** This is an excellent and really cheap ale, and may be made week by week to accumulate a quantity, each fresh brew being put on to part of the lees of the former one, and the surplus yeast thrown away or used for other purposes. If this system is to be followed it pays to obtain a small quantity of true brewer's yeast initially, and it can then be kept going for several months. This bran ale costs about 5p a gallon.

CIDER

Any apples will do, windfall or otherwise, but cider apples or cooking apples are best. Wash them, and then chop them into small pieces with a chopping knife, or crush them with an apple-crusher, or with a piece of heavy timber in a half-tub. Press out the juice with a press or by means of a juice extractor and fill your fermenting vessel. Keep a little spare juice in a separate covered jug for "topping up". After a few days, if kept in a warm place, the juice will start fermenting. The container should be stood on a tray because for a while froth will pour out of the neck of the jar. Wipe this off and keep the jar topped up with the surplus juice. When the ferment quietens wipe the jar and tray clean and fit a fermentation trap. When fermentation has ceased bottle in screw-stopper flagons or strong bottles.

DANDELION BEER

Ingredients:

½ lb.	**Young dandelion plants**	**225 g.**
1 lb.	**Demerara sugar**	**450 g.**
1	**lemon**	
	Yeast	
1 gallon	**Water**	**4.5 litres**
½ oz.	**Root ginger**	**20 g.**
1 oz.	**Cream of tartar**	**30 g.**

Method:

This is a pleasant drink and is said to be good for stomach disorders. The young plants should be lifted in the spring, and well washed. Leave the thick tap roots but remove the fibrous ones. Put the plants, the well bruised ginger and the rind of the lemon (excluding any white pith) in the water and boil for 20 minutes. Strain on to the sugar, the juice of the lemon and cream of tartar, and stir until all is dissolved. Cool to 20°C. (70°F.), add yeast, and ferment (covered) in a warm place for three days. Bottle in screw-stopper bottles.

ELDERFLOWER BEER

Ingredients:

1 pint	**Elderflowers (not pressed down)**	**570 ml.**
1 gallon	**Water**	**4.5 litres**
1	**Lemon**	
1 lb.	**Sugar**	**450 g.**
	Yeast and nutrient	

Method:

Squeeze out the lemon juice and put into a bowl with the elder florets and sugar, then pour over them the boiling water. Infuse for 24 hours, closely covered, then add yeast. Ferment for a week in a warm room, then strain into screw-stopper flagons. Store in a cool place for a week, after which the beer will be ready for drinking.

GINGER BEER

Ingredients:

1 oz.	Root ginger	30 g.
½ oz.	Cream of tartar	20 g.
1 lb.	White sugar	450 g.
1	lemon	
1 gallon	Water	4.5 litres
	Yeast and nutrient	

Method:

The ginger should be crushed and then placed in a bowl with the sugar, cream of tartar and lemon peel (no white pith). Bring the water to the boil and pour it over the ingredients. Stir well to dissolve the sugar, then allow to cool to 20°C. (70°F.) before adding the lemon juice, yeast and nutrient. Cover closely and leave in a warm room for 48 hours, then stir, strain into screw-stopper flagons and store in a cool place. The beer is ready to drink in three to four days.

HONEY BOTCHARD
(a beer-strength mead)

Ingredients:

1 oz.	Hops	30 g.
1¼ lb.	Honey	560 g.
1 gallon	Water	4.5 litres
	Yeast and nutrient	

Method:

Bring the water to the boil, add the hops and honey, and simmer for 30 minutes. Strain the liquid, allow to cool to 20°C. (70°F.) and add yeast and nutrient. Ferment in a warm room for ten days, then siphon into screw-stopper flagons. Store in a cool place for at least a month.

HOW TO START A GINGER BEER PLANT

Grow a Ginger Beer Plant with 2 oz. 55 g. baker's yeast (buy it at a baker's where bread is baked on the premises). Put the yeast into a jar and add 280 ml. (½ pint) water, 2 level teaspoons of sugar, and 2 level teaspoons of ground ginger.

Feed it each day for the next seven to ten days by adding 1 teaspoon of sugar and 1 teaspoon of ground ginger. You will see your "plant" growing day by day.

Strain it. Now strain the mixture through a piece of muslin or a very fine household sieve (keep the sediment) and add to the liquid the juice of 2 lemons, 450 g. (1 lb.) granulated sugar and 570 ml. (1 pint) **boiling** water. Stir until the sugar has dissolved, then make up to one gallon with cold water.

Bottle it. Put the ginger pop into bottles, **filling to about 75 mm (three inches) from the top,** and leave for two hours, taking care not to put them on a stone floor, unless standing on a piece of wood. Then cork **lightly.** Keep for seven to ten days before drinking.

And start again. The sediment you had left when you strained the mixture is divided into two and put into separate glass jars. And you're back in the brewing business again! But now you have two plants instead of one. If one plant is enough for you, give the other to a friend and give him the recipe. To your sediment add half a pint of cold water and carry on as before from "Feed it . . ."

HOP BEER (1)

Ingredients:

5 oz.	**Hops**	**140 g.**
8 gallons	**Water**	
3 lb.	**Brown sugar**	**36 litres**
2 teaspoons	**Granulated yeast and nutrient (level)**	

Method:

Boil the hops and water together slowly for about 40–50 minutes, strain over the sugar, and allow to cool. When tepid add the yeast. Turn into a pan or tub to ferment for four days (at 17°C. (65°F.), up to a week if temperature is lower), then bottle. Crown cork. Can be drunk within a fortnight but may take a month really to clear.

HOP BEER (2)

Ingredients:

$\frac{1}{2}$ **oz.**	**Hops**	**15 g.**
1 lb.	**White sugar**	**450 g.**
$\frac{1}{2}$ **teaspoon**	**Caramel**	
1 gallon	**Water**	**4.5 litres**
$\frac{1}{2}$ **oz.**	**Root ginger (crushed)**	**20 g.**
	Yeast and nutrient	

Method:
Boil all the ingredients except yeast in the water for an hour, and then make up to one gallon if necessary. Strain, cool to 20°C. (70°F.), and add yeast and nutrient. Leave 48 hours in a warm place, closely covered, then siphon off (without disturbing yeast deposit) into screw-stopper flagons, standing them in a cool place. Ready to drink in a week.

NETTLE BEER

Ingredients:

2 gallons	Young nettles	9 litres
$\frac{1}{4}$ oz.	Root ginger	10 g.
4 lb.	Malt	1.8 kg.
1 teaspoon (level)	Granulated yeast	
2 oz.	Hops	50 g.
4 oz.	Sarsaparilla	100 g.
2 gallons	Water	9 litres
$1\frac{1}{2}$ lb.	Sugar	675 g.
2	Lemons	

Method:
Choose young nettle tops. Wash and put into a saucepan with water, ginger, malt, hops and sarsaparilla. Bring to the boil and boil for a quarter of an hour. Put sugar into a large crock or bread pan and strain the liquor on to it; add the juice of the two lemons. Stir until the sugar has dissolved, and allow to cool to 20°C. (70°F.), keeping pan covered, then stir in the yeast. Keep the crock (covered) in a warm room for three days, then strain the beer into bottles, seal or crown cork. Keep the beer in a cool place for a week before drinking—and keep an eye on the stoppers! This makes an excellent summer drink and should be made in May.

146

PARSNIP STOUT

Ingredients:

3½ lb.	Parsnips	1.5 kilo
1 gallon	Water	4.5 litres
1 oz.	Hops	30 g.
½ lb.	Malt extract	225 g.
	Yeast	
1 tablespoon	Caramel gravy browning *or* ¼ lb. black malt	
1¼ lb.	Demerara sugar	560 g.

Method:

Scrub the parsnips, slice them in 10 mm. (½ in.) slices. Bring the water to the boil, add the parsnips, hops, and caramel colouring (or black malt) and boil for 20 minutes, then strain on to the malt extract and sugar. Stir well to dissolve. Cool to 20°C. (70°F.) then add yeast and nutrient, cover well, and leave in a warm place for seven days. Then siphon into screw-stopper flagons and store in a cool larder for a fortnight before drinking.

SPRUCE BEER

To make the beer the recipe is as follows:

Melt 1 kilo (2 lb.) sugar, treacle, essence of malt, molasses, or honey, into a 4.5 litre (1 gallon) of hot water, put into fermentation bin, add another 4.5 litres of cold water and 2 tablespoonfuls of the essence of spruce. Spruce essence can be purchased from winemaking supplies firms and from some branches of principal chain chemists. When the must is tepid add ale yeast. Ferment for three days, then bottle. It will be ready for use within one week.

TREACLE ALE

Ingredients:

½ lb.	Golden Syrup	225 g.
½ lb.	Black treacle	225 g.
½ lb.	Demerara sugar	225 g.
1 oz.	Hops	30 g.
1 gallon	Water	4.5 litres
	Yeast and nutrient	

Method:

Bring the water to the boil, add the hops, syrup, treacle and sugar, and simmer for 45 minutes. Strain, cool to 70°F., add yeast and nutrient, and ferment for at least a week before bottling in screw-stopper flagons.

COCK ALE

In a 100-year-old book on brewing we came across the following recipe for a fearsome brew, "Cock Ale":

"Take 10 gallons of ale and a large cock, the older the better; parboil the cock, flay him, and stamp him in a stone mortar until his bones are broken (you must draw and gut him when you flay him), then put the cock into two quarts of sack, and put to it five pounds of raisins of the sun, stoned; some blades of mace, and a few cloves; put all these into a canvas bag, and a little before you find the ale has been working, put the bag and ale together into a vessel. In a week or nine days bottle it up; fill the bottle just above the neck, and give it the same time to ripen as other ale."

Rather amusedly, and entirely by way of experiment, it was decided to try this, on a one-gallon quantity. Astonishingly, it made an excellent ale, nourishing and strong-flavoured, of the "barley wine" type.

Many years later we heard of the old West Country practice of putting a joint of meat into a barrel of cider—where it disappeared—in order to produce a really strong brew. And that it had been discovered that there was in fact a good scientific basis for this, in that it greatly increased the protein content of the brew! So it's worth trying.

All you need are some pieces of cooked chicken, and a few chicken bones, all well crushed or minced (about a tenth of the eatable portion of the bird), half a pound of raisins, a very little mace, and one (or, if you like, two) cloves. Soak these for 24 hours in half a bottle of your strongest white country wine.

Then make one gallon of beer as described in our malt extract section using 1 lb. malt extract, 1 oz. hops, ½ lb. Demerara sugar, 1 gallon water, yeast and nutrient. Add the whole of your cock mixture to the fermenting must, to the fermenting wort at the end of the second day. Fermentation will last six or seven days longer than usual and the ale should be matured at least a month in bottle.

CHAPTER 14

Serving Your Beers

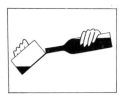

The rule is: drink when clear, serve cool. There is bound to be some sediment, which will cloud the drink if carelessly poured. Take a quart jug and have it by your hand, or set out your two pint tankards or four smaller glasses so that you can pour continuously without having to return the bottle to the vertical. Open the bottle—with caution; you may have over-primed the bottle.

Hold the jug or other receptacle at a slant in one hand and gently tilt the bottle in the other, so that the beer slides out slowly against the side of it.

Avoid the uneven flow that comes of pouring too fast; it will stir up the sediment. Watch the colour of the beer as you pour and stop the flow smartly as soon as you see it becoming cloudy. You will be left with a couple of inches of yeasty beer in the bottom of the bottle. Drink it down yourself and know what good health is, or pour it into a spare flagon, as already suggested, with other dregs to settle. If you bungle the pouring and the drink is cloudy don't apologise. You are only giving others a share in the most nourishing part of the brew, instead of keeping if for yourself!

"LIVELY" BEER

Sometimes in spring or summer, usually at the onset of a warm spell, you will get an extra vigorous fermentation in the flagon, so that the beer is over-"lively". When you unscrew a stopper there may even be a "pheep!" instead of a gentle hiss and the beer will foam out vigorously. At times it will send up a spout of foaming beer like a fountain, to the detriment of the ceiling and paintwork! And (what is perhaps even worse, in a beer drinker's opinion) all the yeast sediment will rise so much as to make the beer horribly cloudy and undrinkable.

There is only one solution. Wipe all the bottles clean and stand them in the sink. Then release the stoppers and let the bottles foam naturally. Let the process continue until no more froth issues from the bottles (although there may still be a head inside them) then screw down once more, wipe the bottles clean, and store for 48 hours, by which time the beer will be clear again, and drinkable, its liveliness normal.

Not much beer will be lost, except in severe cases, for usually only foam issues, but even this can be saved and poured back into the bottles if you stand the flagons in a clean bowl (not one which has held detergent) or half cask and collect the overflow.

Another way is to insert a cork and length of tubing into each bottle and drain off the froth into fresh containers as publicans do with casks which are too lively.

EXHIBITING AND JUDGING

Brewing has now attained the same stature as winemaking as regards competitions, for the National Guild of Wine and Beer Judges now includes a most useful chapter on beer judging in its handbook for judges, show organisers, and competitors (*Judging Home Made Wines and Beers*) which will well repay reading.

The Guild sets out the main types of beer, and their characteristics, and explains what the judge will be looking for—clean, sound bottles; clean stoppers with sound rubber washers, an air space of $\frac{1}{2}$ inch to $\frac{3}{4}$ inch, a firm yeast deposit, if any, a good head and head retention, coupled with a small and lively "bead" (the bubbles), a satisfactory aroma, and the correct body and flavour for that particular type of beer. Normally points will be awarded as follows: 2 for bottling, 4 for bouquet, 4 for condition and clarity, and 20 for taste and flavour.

You may care not only to become an exhibitor, but eventually to become a judge as well, for judges are in great demand; again, the handbook will be your guide to success, and you will eventually be able to take the Guild's qualifying examination.

Other Amateur Winemaker Books

FIRST STEPS IN WINEMAKING
The acknowledged introduction to the subject. Unbeatable at the price.
C. J. J. Berry £2.00, p. & p. 71p

SCIENTIFIC WINEMAKING – made easy
The most advanced and practical textbook on the subject.
J. R. Mitchell, L.I.R.C., A.I.F.S.T. £2.00, p. & p. 40p

WINEMAKING AND BREWING
The theory and practice of winemaking and brewing in detail.
Dr. F. W. Beech and Dr. A. Pollard £1.10, p. & p. 40p

"AMATEUR WINEMAKER" RECIPES
Fascinatingly varied collection of over 200 recipes.
C. J. J. Berry £2.00, p. & p. 51p

WINEMAKING WITH CANNED AND DRIED FRUIT
How to make delightful wines from off the supermarket shelf.
C. J. J. Berry £2.00, p. & p. 33p

130 NEW WINEMAKING RECIPES
Superb collection of up-to-date recipes.
C. J. J. Berry £1.80, p. & p. 44p

RECIPES FOR PRIZEWINNING WINES
Produce superb wines for your own satisfaction!
Bryan Acton £2.00, p. & p. 37p

WHYS AND WHEREFORES OF WINEMAKING
Assists the winemaker to *understand* what he is doing.
£1.50, p. & p. 29p

THE WINEMAKER'S DICTIONARY
190 pages of quick reference to all the questions a winemaker sometimes has to ask. Ideal companion for First Steps in Winemaking.
Peter McCall £2.00, p. & p. 51p

HOW TO MAKE WINES WITH A SPARKLE
Discover the secrets of producing Champagne-like wine of superb quality.
J. Restall and D. Hebbs £2.00, p. & p. 37p

PROGRESSIVE WINEMAKING

500-pages, from scientific theory to the production of quality wines at home.

Peter Duncan and Bryan Acton   £3.00, p. & p. 65p

BREWING BEERS LIKE THOSE YOU BUY

Over 100 original recipes to enable you to imitate famous beers from around the world. Full instructions for the beginner.

Dave Line   £2.00, p. & p. 42p

JUDGING HOME MADE WINES

National Guild of Judges official handbook.

£2.00, p. & p. 25p

WORLDWIDE WINEMAKING RECIPES

An intriguing book of recipes ranging from prickly pears to paw paws to lychees and logans.

Roy Ekins   £1.00, p. & p. 29p

QUICKIE TABLE WINES

Well illustrated pamphlet enabling anyone to make highly satisfactory table wines in 4–5 weeks.

Ben Bennetts   60p, p. & p. 23p

THE HAPPY BREWER

Caters for the home brewer who wishes to go more deeply into the theory of brewing.

Wilf Newsom   £1.00, p. & p. 29p

COMMONSENSE WINEMAKING

A practical no frills primer in winemaking and with its aid anyone can quickly and easily be making superb wines.

Anne Parrack   £1.50, p. & p. 40p

BEER KITS AND BREWING

A much needed up-to-date book on home brewing. All the latest information on beer kits, hopped worts, malt extract and new equipment. Popular pressure barrels and gas injection systems described – 50 new exciting recipes.

Dave Line   £1.60, p. & p. 51p

HOME BREWING FOR AMERICANS

Straightforward illustrated book, presenting a simple method of brewing using American malts, equipment and ingredients available in N. America to produce quality beers popular in America.

David Miller   £1.50, p. & p. 37p

MAKING WINES LIKE THOSE YOU BUY
Imitate commercial wines at a fraction of what they would cost to buy.
Bryan Acton and Peter Duncan £2.00, p. & p. 46p

THE BIG BOOK OF BREWING
The most comprehensive book available on mashing "true beers".
Dave Line £2.50, p. & p. 65p

MAKING INEXPENSIVE LIQUEURS
The liqueur lover's handbook.
Ren Bellis £2.20, p. & p. 51p

WOODWORK FOR WINEMAKERS
Make your own wine press, fermentation cupboard, fruit pulper, bottle racks, etc.
C. J. Dart and D. A. Smith £2.00, p. & p. 37p

BREWING BETTER BEERS
Explains many finer points of brewing technique.
Ken Shales £1.50, p. & p. 44p

HINTS ON HOME BREWING
Concise and basic down to earth instructions on home brewing.
C. J. J. Berry 60p, p. & p. 22p

MAKING MEAD
The only full-length paperback available on this winemaking speciality.
Bryan Acton and Peter Duncan £1.80, p. & p. 29p

EXPRESS WINE MAKING
If you wish to use your own selected ingredients and make good sound wines, yet have them ready for drinking in a month (or less). This is the book for you.
Ren Bellis £1.00, p. & p. 37p

MAKING CIDER
The only book available on this fascinating and ultra British craft.
Jo Deal £1.50, p. & p. 29p

100 WINEMAKING PROBLEMS ANSWERED
The author gives full, scientific and accurate explanations of and answers to a hundred of the most commonly encountered problems.
Cedric Austin £1.60, p. & p. 29p

DIABETIC BREWING AND WINEMAKING
Is it safe? How much? Can a diabetic brew beer and wine? All the answers plus many recipes.

Dr. Peter McCall £1.50, p. & p. 37p

WINEMAKING WITH CONCENTRATES
Using American and European concentrates to make delicious wines and using less sugar in the process.

Peter Duncan £1.50, p. & p. 33p

WINES FROM YOUR VINES
The logical sequence to Mr. Poulter's first book "Growing Vines". Readable and very practical, covering all aspects of winemaking from grapes.

N. Poulter £2.00, p. & p. 37p

VINES IN YOUR GARDEN
This fully illustrated booklet is a must for those with a little garden space, who wish to make their own wine and eat their own grapes.

James Page-Roberts £1.00, p. & p. 20p

ALL ABOUT BEER
The Brewing process described to home brewing terms.

Bob Pritchard £2.50, p. & p. 51p

GREAT FERMENTATIONS
The honest record of an enthusiastic hobbyist's very individual approach to the subject.

Marion Whittow £2.00, p. & p. 44p

MODERN WINEMAKING TECHNIQUES
This book details the method of juice extraction and how to obtain the best results from a wide range of ingredients.

Gladys Blacklock £2.00, p. & p. 44p

WINEMAKING WITH ELDERBERRIES
A new book which gives you all the fascinating background about, and a wealth of recipes for using, *sambucus nigra*.

T. Edwin Belt £1.75, p. & p. 37p

BE A WINE AND BEER JUDGE
— there are many proficient winemakers, and perhaps exhibitors who have toyed with the idea of becoming an officially recognised wine judge, but just do not know where to start, or how to qualify. This book tells them how.

S. W. (Andy) Andrews £1.00, p. & p. 29p

154

GROWING VINES

Down-to-earth book for the viticulturist.

N. Poulter £2.00, p. & p. 37p

Prices of all goods below include VAT

BINDERS

De luxe binders for your copies of the *Amateur Winemaker*
£1.86, p. & p. £1.10p

TIES

Vintners — Black, green-brown.
Brewers — Red, brown-blue.

£2.75, inc. p. & p.

Please state colour when ordering

WINE LOG

For recording all your wine making.
Cover with 25 cards £2.08, p. & p. 40p
Cover with 50 cards £2.45, p. & p. 54p
25 cards 37p, p. & p. 23p
100 cards £1.43, p. & p. 47p

DIPLOMAS

12p each plus p. & p.

The Amateur Winemaker, South Street, Andover, Hants. SP10 2BU

INDEX

158

164

167

EST. 1958

BEERBRITE CAPS

WHAT NEW ADVANTAGES CAN THEY ACHIEVE?

*A clear bottled beer without a yeast deposit! Never before possible!

*Commercial standards of clarity can be achieved

*They can be used with the beer of your choice

*Bottled beer can be transported for picnics, fishing trips or numerous other social occasions

*Bottles can be opened by friends as they would normally open Commercial beers

*Beers of higher quality can be achieved due to correct conditioning in the bottle

*Crown Corks can be safely used in conjunction with Beerbrite Caps

*The bottle life of the beer is extended by this method

*The final presentation can reach the highest Commercial standard

S.V. BOTTLE ANGLE BRACKET

SUPERBREW

THE COMPLETE HOME BREW KIT

No additional sugar required

PALE ALE · LAGER · BITTER · STOUT BARLEY WINE

These 4lb. kits contain ALL that you need to make first class beer.
Edme have incorporated the necessary amount of proper brewing sugar with malt and hops for the type of beer to be brewed and concentrated them to a complete kit. You simply open the can, dissolve the contents in water, add the yeast provided under the cap, and ferment.

Also available are the well-known Edme malt extracts and hopped concentrates for home brewing.

Write for free descriptive leaflet of the complete Edme range showing recipes and methods.

Available from home brew depts., of larger Boots' Stores and home brew shops everywhere.

EDME

THE CHOICE OF THE FIRST-CLASS BREWER

EDME
SUPERBREW
BITTER
the complete home brew kit
No need to add sugar - makes 24 pints

EDME LTD. MISTLEY, MANNINGTREE, ESSEX. TEL: 0206 39 2232

The
⟨○ BREWMAKER ○⟩
range of beers
now caters for
everybodys' taste,
pocket & thirst !

Southampton Homebrews Ltd., First Avenue, Millbrook, Southampton.